NARCISSIST

a **COMPLETE GUIDE** *for* **DEALING WITH NARCISSISM** *and* **CREATING** *the* **LIFE YOU WANT**

JUDY DYER

Narcissist: A Complete Guide for Dealing with Narcissism
and Creating the Life You Want
by Judy Dyer

© Copyright 2019 by Judy Dyer

All Rights Reserved.

Disclaimer: This book is designed to provide accurate and authoritative information in regard to the subject matter covered. By its sale, neither the publisher nor the author is engaged in rendering psychological or other professional services. If expert assistance or counseling is needed, the services of a competent professional should be sought.

ISBN-10: 1702189732
ISBN-13: 978-1702189736

ALSO BY JUDY DYER

*Empath: A Complete Guide for Developing Your Gift
and Finding Your Sense of Self*

*The Highly Sensitive: How to Stop Emotional Overload,
Relieve Anxiety, and Eliminate Negative Energy*

Empath and The Highly Sensitive: 2 in 1 Bundle

*The Empowered Empath: A Simple Guide on Setting
Boundaries, Controlling Your Emotions, and Making Life Easier*

Empaths and Narcissists: 2 in 1 Bundle

*Borderline Personality Disorder: A Complete BPD Guide for
Managing Your Emotions and Improving Your Relationships*

CONTENTS

Introduction 7

Your Free Gift - Heyoka Empath 13

Chapter 1:   A Narcissist – How to Recognize One 19

Chapter 2:   What Causes Narcissism? 36

Chapter 3:   Gaslighting – A Form of Narcissist Abuse 45

Chapter 4:   What to do When Your Parent is
             a Narcissist 61

Chapter 5:   Empaths and Narcissists – The Toxic Couple 74

Chapter 6:   Why Victims Stay – Emotional and
             Psychological Reasons 81

Chapter 7:   Protection Strategy: How to Break Free
             From a Narcissist 95

Chapter 8:   Protection Strategy: How to Slowly
             Detach Yourself From a Narcissist 103

Chapter 9:   Protection Strategy: How to Create
             Boundaries with a Narcissist 107

Chapter 10: Protection Strategy: How to Stop an
             Argument With a Narcissist 115

Chapter 11: Protection Strategy: Practice Giving
             Balanced Love 119

Chapter 12: Protection Strategy: Cut All Psychic Cords ... 122

Chapter 13: Protection Strategy: Reclaim Your Life 126

Chapter 14: Dating Again 137

Chapter 15: Frequently Asked Questions about
Narcissists 140

Conclusion 144

INTRODUCTION

You will hear the word "narcissism" touted about as if it's the latest fashion statement; however, what some people don't realize is that it's actually a serious psychological disorder that seriously affects the individual and the people who are exposed to this vicious personality type. A study conducted by the San Diego State University concluded that it is possible that there is an "epidemic of narcissism" among the youth in the United States. The researchers determined that celebrity culture, permissive parenting, and the internet have all contributed to this phenomenon. ABC News filmed a news story entitled "The Rise of Narcissism in America," and psychologist Dr. Jean M. Twenge wrote a book based on the San Diego State University study, which highlighted that over the last two decades there has been a 67 percent increase in narcissism. She also estimated that approximately 10 percent of the population suffers from narcissistic personality disorder (NPD).

The bad news is that there is a high possibility that you are working with, living with, or in a relationship with someone who has some level of NPD. Even though this is unsettling, the good news is that you are not alone in this situation and neither do you have to stay in it.

From Greek mythology to the psychology of the modern world, our understanding of narcissism has developed immensely. The condition has been considered untreatable for many years; however, over the last forty years, mental health professionals have started to identify successful ways to treat and manage the condition.

Disclaimer: You will notice that throughout this book, I refer to the narcissist as a "he," this is for no other reason other than for the sake of consistency. Although statistics do state that the majority of narcissists are males, there are also plenty of narcissistic women.

JOIN OUR SUPPORT GROUP

In order to maximize the value you receive from this book, I highly encourage you to join our tight-knit community on Facebook. Here you will be able to connect and share strategies with others dealing with narcissists in order to continue your growth.

Taking this journey alone is not recommended, and this can be an excellent support network for you.

It would be great to connect with you there,

Judy Dyer

To Join, Visit: www.pristinepublish.com/empathgroup

Or Scan the QR Code on Your Phone:

DOWNLOAD THE AUDIO VERSION OF THIS BOOK FREE

If you love listening to audiobooks on-the-go or would enjoy a narration as you read along, I have great news for you. You can download the audiobook version of Narcissist for FREE (Regularly $14.95) just by signing up for a FREE 30-day audible trial!

Visit: www.pristinepublish.com/audiobooks

Or Scan the QR Code on Your Phone:

YOUR FREE GIFT - HEYOKA EMPATH

A lot of empaths feel trapped, as if they've hit a glass ceiling they can't penetrate. They know there's another level to their gift, but they can't seem to figure out what it is. They've read dozens of books, been to counselling, and confided in other experienced empaths, but that glass ceiling remains. They feel alone, and alienated from the rest of the world because they know they've got so much more to give, but can't access it. Does this sound like you?

The inability to connect to your true and authentic self is a tragedy. Being robbed of the joy of embracing the full extent of your humanity is a terrible misfortune. The driving force of human nature is to live according to one's own sense of self, values, and emotions. Since the beginning of time, philosophers, writers, and scholars have argued that authenticity is one of the most important elements of an individual's well-being.

When there's a disconnect between a person's inner being and their expressions, it can be psychologically damaging. Heyokas are the most powerful type of empaths, and many of them are not fully aware of who they are. While other empaths experience feelings of overwhelm and exhaustion from absorbing others' energy and emotions, heyoka empaths experience an additional aspect of exhaustion in that they are fighting a constant battle with their inability to be completely authentic.

The good news is that the only thing stopping you from becoming your authentic self is a lack of knowledge. You need to know exactly who you are so you can tap into the resources that have been lying dormant within you. In this bonus e-book, you'll gain in-depth information about the seven signs that you're a heyoka empath, and why certain related abilities are such powerful traits. You'll find many of the answers to the questions you've been searching for your entire life such as:

- Why you feel uncomfortable when you're around certain people
- How you always seem to find yourself on the right path even though your decisions are not based on logic or rationale
- The reason you get so offended when you find out others have lied to you
- Why you analyze everything in such detail
- The reason why humor is such an important part of your life
- Why you refuse to follow the crowd, regardless of the consequences
- The reason why strangers and animals are drawn to you

There are three main components to authenticity: understanding who you are, expressing who you are, and letting the world experience who you are. Your first step on this journey is to know who you are, and with these seven signs that you're a heyoka empath, you'll find out. I've included snippets about the first three signs in this description to give you full confidence that you're on the right track:

Sign 1: You Feel and Understand Energy

Heyoka empaths possess a natural ability to tap into energy. They can walk into a room and immediately discern the atmosphere. When an individual walks past them, they can literally see into their soul because they can sense the aura that person is carrying. But empaths also understand their own energy, and they allow it to guide them. You will often hear this ability referred to as "the sixth sense." The general consensus is that only a few people have this gift. But the reality is that everyone was born with the ability to feel energy; it's just been demonized and turned into something spooky, when in actual fact, it's the most natural state to operate in.

Sign 2: You are Led by Your Intuition

Do you find that you just know things? You don't spend hours, days, and weeks agonizing over decisions, you can just feel that something is the right thing to do, and you go ahead and do it. That's because you're led by your intuition and you're connected to the deepest part of yourself. You know your soul, you listen to it, and you trust it. People like Oprah Winfrey, Steve Jobs and Richard Branson followed their intuition steadfastly and it led them to become some of the most successful people in the history of the world.

Living from within is the way we were created to be, and those who trust this ability will find their footing in life a lot more quickly than others. Think of it as a GPS system: when it's been programmed properly, it will always take you to your destination via the fastest route.

Sign 3: You Believe in Complete Honesty

In general, empaths don't like being around negative energy, and there's nothing that can shift a positive frequency faster than dishonesty. Anything that isn't the truth is a lie, even the tiny ones that we excuse away as "white lies." And as soon as they're released from someone's mouth, so is negative energy. Living an authentic life requires complete honesty at all times, and although the truth may hurt, it's better than not being able to trust someone. Heyoka empaths get very uncomfortable in the presence of liars. They are fully aware that the vibrations of the person don't match the words they are saying. Have you ever experienced a brain freeze mid-conversation? All of a sudden you just couldn't think straight, you couldn't articulate yourself properly, and things just got really awkward? That's because your empath antenna picked up on a lie.

Heyoka Empath: 7 Signs You're A Heyoka Empath & Why It's So Powerful is a revolutionary tool that will help you transition from uncertainty to complete confidence in who you are. In this easy-to-read guide, I will walk you through exactly what makes you a heyoka empath. I've done the research for you, so no more spending hours, days, weeks, and even years searching for answers, because everything you need is right here in this book.

You have a deep need to share yourself with the world, but you've been too afraid because you knew something was missing. The information within the pages of this book is the missing piece in the jigsaw puzzle of your life. There's no turning back now!

Get *Heyoka Empath* for Free by Visiting

www.pristinepublish.com/empathbonus

Or Scan the QR Code on Your Phone:

CHAPTER 1

A NARCISSIST – HOW TO RECOGNIZE ONE

Once upon a time, there lived a handsome young Greek man, he was a hunter and the son of Cephissus the river god. He had many admirers; all the women loved him and would throw themselves at him; however, he showed no appreciation towards them, only contempt and disdain. One day, while Narcissus was searching for food in the woods, Echo, the Oread nymph saw him and fell in love with him and started following him. Narcissus sensed that he was being watched and Echo revealed herself and attempted to hug him. He shoved her out of his way and told her to get out of his space. Echo was devastated, her heart was completely crushed and as a result, she ended up living as a wanderer in the woods for the remainder of her life, until she disintegrated and all that was left of her was an echo.

Nemesis was the goddess of revenge and retribution, and when she found out what had happened, she took Narcissus to a river and made him look at his reflection, he fell in love with himself but didn't realize that it was only a reflection. Once he came to the conclusion that there was nothing he could do about the love that he was feeling, he became depressed and killed himself.

The mythology of Narcissus is where the term narcissism originated; however, it wasn't coined until the end of the nineteenth century. The story is a reflection of how today's narcissistic relationship plays out. Narcissus was too concerned with himself to notice that someone genuinely wanted to love him, and Echo desperately wanted to be heard, only to be pushed to the side. There are several versions of the story, and in one of them, Narcissus is so prideful that when someone tries to love him, he is horrified. He hears what Echo has to say but shouts at her to be quiet. Just as in a relationship with a narcissist today, the woman will often aggravate her partner to anger when she says or does something that he doesn't agree with. Just as the mythological story reveals, a narcissistic person is destructive to himself and to those who have a desire to love him.

Character Traits of a Narcissist

- Little to no compassion or empathy for the feelings, opinions, and thoughts of others
- Demeans and belittles others to enforce their superiority
- Self-absorbed in their own problems and thoughts
- Has no respect or regard for authority
- Finds it difficult to deal with criticism
- Exploits people to gain exceptionalism and power or to make themselves feel that they are better than others

- Prone to outbursts of rage
- Lies and distorts the truth to support their own interests, perceptions, and goals
- Incapable of admitting when they are wrong
- Extreme jealousy
- As well as being emotionally abusive, the narcissist is also capable of physically abusing their partner

There is absolutely nothing wrong with having high confidence levels. At the end of the day, if you don't love yourself, who is going to love you? Everyone wants to be admired by friends, family, and loved ones for the things that they have achieved. However, when loving thy self turns into an obsession, it's time to get a little concerned. Self-love can become so obsessive, that you act as if you are the only person who exists on the planet and you have zero compassion for others. This type of attitude leads to abuse and other destructive behaviors that are detrimental to the individual and those around them.

EXPLAINING NARCISSISM

In 1898, British psychologist Havelock Ellis was the first to tell the story of Narcissus as a description of pathological self-absorption. The terms "narcissistic" and "narcissist" were soon picked up by other psychologists, and the words were popularized after Sigmund Freud wrote a report on the condition in 1914.

There is more to narcissism than having an inflated sense of self and being conceited and egotistical. Yes, these are all unattractive qualities when they are in the extreme; however, true narcissism involves a maniacal pursuit of praise, ambition, and gratification. Those who suffer from the slightest degree of NPD can be arrogant, smug, and vain and have an unusually high level of self-esteem. This is their outward appearance, but deep down they are extremely insecure and feel as if they have little self-worth. They thrive off admiration from others, which is how they feed their belief that they are more important than anyone else. Psychologists refer to this as "narcissistic supply," and it is almost like a drug for the narcissist. They are addicted to receiving confirmation that they are indeed superior beings. Typically, narcissists don't have an empathetic bone in their body, which basically means that they don't have a care in the world for anyone apart from themselves.

There are different degrees of narcissism; in fact, psychologists believe that we are all slightly narcissistic. It is even possible that narcissism is required as a method of survival in the world today. Being a little egotistical can be beneficial; however, the behavior of a fully narcissistic individual is very destructive.

According to the Diagnostic and Statistical Manual of Mental Disorders, to be considered narcissistic, a person's behavior must fall into the following categories:

- They blow situations out of proportion and are incapable of putting things into perspective.
- The narcissist is unable to empathize with the feelings or thoughts of others.

- The narcissist is only concerned with their own issues.
- The narcissist has no respect for authority.
- Deep down the narcissist feels inferior and will compensate by doing everything they can to be seen as superior.
- The narcissist is incapable of receiving constructive criticism.
- The narcissist needs sexual admiration and is often an exhibitionist.
- The narcissist is vain, exploitative, and dependent on others.

To a certain degree, all people who have been diagnosed with NPD exhibit these traits. However, there are also other types of narcissistic behaviors. Since the 1950s, there has been a dramatic increase in the number of people who suffer from narcissism. During this time, therapists have noticed that there are variations in the condition, which have been divided into several categories. Narcissism in children is typically a result of learned behavior from their primary caregivers and can be unlearned. Therefore, psychologists are reluctant to diagnose children with NPD. Fully-fledged NPD only exists in adults and is treated differently; other types of narcissism include the following.

- **The Phallic Narcissist:** These are typically males who have a great love for themselves and their physical bodies. They strut like roosters and are very aggressive and athletic. They are exhibitionists who enjoy putting their bodies on display.

- **The Manipulative Narcissist:** They enjoy manipulating and influencing others. The manipulative narcissist feeds their need for power by manipulating, bullying, lying, and intimidating others.

- **The Paranoid Narcissist:** The paranoid narcissist suffers from a deep self-hatred; they project this onto others with extreme jealous behavior, and they are overly sensitive to criticism.

- **The Craving Narcissist:** Although narcissists are extremely egotistical, craving narcissists are very needy, demanding of love, emotionally clingy, and attention-seeking.

The most significant personality trait of a narcissist is grandiosity. This is not the same as boasting or pridefulness, it is an unrealistic inflated sense of self. If a person won't stop going on about how they were the MVP of their college basketball team at a dinner party, it might show that that individual is boastful, conceited, or even a little ill-mannered. This can be extremely annoying; however, it isn't narcissistic if it is true. But if the person did not even play on the team but sat on the bench all season, that is being grandiose.

MILLION'S SUBTYPES

American psychologist Theodore Million is renowned for his pioneering work in identifying personality disorders. In his work, he has included several subtypes to narcissistic personality disorder.

- **The Amorous Narcissist:** The main characteristic of the amorous narcissist is an obsession with seduction and erotica—this is a subtype of the manipulative narcissist. They use sex appeal and sex as a weapon for power and control. This illusion of power is not restricted to the opposite sex, they believe that they can also use it against the same sex.

- **The Elitist Narcissist:** Displays the same characteristics of the phallic narcissist but is also female.

- **The Compensatory Narcissist:** Compensates for their deep feelings of low self-esteem and inadequacy by using narcissistic supply. They seek to build up an image of high self-worth by creating an illusion of superiority.

- **The Unprincipled Narcissist:** This type of narcissism is characterized by deliberate deception and pathological lying to obtain narcissistic supply. They are typically abusive conmen who are unscrupulous and deceptive.

- **The Fanatic Narcissist:** They love themselves so much that they think they are on the same level of a deity. They battle with low self-esteem and try to cover it up with extreme delusions of grandeur.

NARCISSISTS, PSYCHOPATHS, AND SOCIOPATHS

Narcissists are often referred to as psychopaths or sociopaths, which is not entirely true, although they do share similar character traits. According to criminology and sociology professor Dr. Scott Bonn, psychopaths, and sociopaths suffer from antisocial behavior disorder. They both have a complete disregard for the law, are callous, refuse to accept responsibility for their actions, lack empathy, have no respect for the rights of others, can be exceptionally violent, sexually promiscuous, and shallow. Narcissists also share these traits.

However, psychopaths often have a long and varied criminal history, whereas narcissists have a tendency to commit psychological and emotional transgressions in the way they slander, sabotage, and devalue the lives of their victims. They are capable of showing guilt or remorse, whereas psychopaths and sociopaths are often incapable due to their lack of empathy and self-absorption. Brain scans have revealed that both narcissists and psychopaths have brain abnormalities. Narcissists show structural abnormalities in the areas of the brain that deal with compassion, and psychopaths in the areas that deal with guilt and moral reasoning.

Narcissists have an unhealthy need for validation, but sociopaths and psychopaths are not concerned with it. Narcissists take advantage of people they are threatened by, whereas sociopaths do so simply because they enjoy it. However, when it comes to the callous nature in which they treat people, they are very similar and get sadistic pleasure out of harming people. This is because they have a desire for power and control, and since they are unable to experience the full range of human emotions, they get their pleasure out of traumatizing their victims.

YOU WILL NEVER TRULY KNOW A NARCISSIST

One of the most important lessons you must learn about a narcissist is that you will never truly know who they are. This is because the person you see in front of you isn't who they are behind closed doors. The narcissist will present themselves as successful, kind, generous, an intimate partner, intelligent, and charming. They are typically very well-loved people. However, they reveal their true colors to their partners, which is when they become cruel, selfish, abusive, hateful, lacking empathy, and having a tendency to step outside of the relationship. They will do things like make up situations to make it look as if the partner is needy and insane.

One common misconception about narcissists is that they are all extremely successful, accomplished, and powerful, but this is not always the case. Some of them are not very successful and have perhaps failed at life, and this can make them quite vulnerable. Although they will put on a display of superiority to hide their deep-rooted feelings of insecurity. Whether they are ultra-successful or living on the threshold of poverty, narcissists come in all shapes and sizes.

You will also find narcissists in philanthropic and charitable positions; for example, you will find them working as pastors in churches and as social workers. They actually thrive on taking positions where they will be able to execute their power. You will find counselors and mental health professionals who suffer from narcissistic personality disorder. They intentionally take on these positions, pretending to be empathetic when they don't have a compassionate bone in their body so that they have access to more victims. No matter the profession or social status, narcissists are very dangerous people with zero empathy. They believe that they are entitled to what they are not entitled to and they have no desire to change their behavior.

NARCISSISTS – THE TRUE SELF AND THE FALSE SELF

The narcissist supply is a term used to describe the admiration and attention they get from their victims. They care nothing for the people they target, and they target people for one reason only—narcissistic supply. They need this because they are incapable of connecting with others emotionally. It is also a form of entertainment for them because narcissists have the tendency to get exceptionally bored. Nothing entertains them more than to watch others suffer.

The narcissist sees their victims as some sort of accessory, like a piece of furniture or a handbag. Because they are lacking in the full range of human emotions, they lack the ability to understand that the people they are hurting have desires, wants, and needs. They have a fear of intimacy because getting close to someone would expose their true and unbearable character. They are good at faking their emotions and will often turn on the waterworks with great ease. They have a chameleon-like character and can adapt to what they think the other person wants or needs. They do this for manipulation purposes only, so they can get what they want out of their victims. They have what is referred to as "cold empathy," a psychological condition where a person is capable of having an intellectual understanding of what a person is going through, but they don't connect with the feelings. Even when they cry and act as if they feel remorseful, they only do so to get out of taking responsibility for their actions.

When narcissists get into a relationship, they lure their partners in with a false sense of security and intimacy. Their characters are very attractive which is why they are able to rope people in the way they do. A study conducted in 2015 found that women who desire to get married are typically attracted to narcissistic type personalities due to their charming nature, ability to provide, and social status. Despite their reputation for being so destructive in relationships, they are still viewed as desirable partners.

To those on the outside looking in, the narcissist is the kindest, most generous, at times spiritual and in-touch person. It is only those closest to them—their victims—that see the true evil side of a narcissist. Similar to psychopaths and sociopaths, narcissists create a shield of a charming, alluring and sweet demeanor to trap their victims in a web of splendor. This is how they get away with their behavior— nobody is going to believe that they are capable of such heinous actions. The victims are even led to question their sanity because the narcissist is capable of easily switching from nice to nasty in the blink of an eye. This makes the experience for the victim even more traumatic because they are just not sure if what they are experiencing is real. The reality of the situation is that the evil side of the narcissist is their true self, and the nice side is the façade.

When narcissists are wearing their mask, they are capable of fooling anyone including highly intelligent, educated, and successful people. No one is perfect, but most people don't go out of their way to make other people's lives miserable, so you just don't expect other people to do that. Victims would rather believe in the mask and just hope that the narcissist is just having a bad day when they show their dark side. Accepting that someone is just wicked is a difficult thing to do. It can take a significant amount of time before the cognitive dissonance in a victim is resolved when trapped in this type of relationship. What happens is that the victim develops conflicting thoughts, feelings, and beliefs about the abusive partner who is basically living a double life. To resolve cognitive dissonance, the solution lies in accepting that the abuse is taking place as opposed to denying or rationalizing it, which is a common response when victims develop a bond with their abusers.

To begin the process of disentangling yourself from the stronghold of narcissist abuse, you must first accept that narcissists do not feel any type of empathy for their victims. They simply do not care how you feel. The only type of feeling they may experience is referred to as "narcissistic injury," this is the despair and rage they feel when they are criticized, or when a person threatens their false sense of entitlement and superiority. This gives them a desperate need to protect their false selves even more. What I am trying to say is that there is no point in attempting to make a narcissist feel any type of remorse because their brains are not wired to do so. They will do anything to protect who they really are, which is why it is a waste of time to try to get the narcissist to see things through your eyes. Their main aim is to protect their true character by any means necessary.

So how do narcissists manage to deceive people the way they do? The reality is that they are capable of taking on multiple different personalities to get what they want from their audience. They will become who you need them to become to get their supply of attention, praise, sex, money, or whatever else it is that they want from their victim. They are also very good at projection and do a very good job of convincing their victims that they are the crazy ones and that their perception of reality is inaccurate. Narcissists have mastered the art of manipulation so well that the victims manipulate themselves into believing that what they are experiencing, hearing, seeing, thinking, and feeling is wrong. They can make you believe that the nasty comment they made was just a joke and they didn't really mean it or that the affair they've been having for the past six weeks was just a one-off and that's not who they really are. Narcissists are pathological liars who twist reality as if it's a normal part of everyday life to mask the true nature of their sadistic agenda.

It is of no surprise that the victims of narcissist abuse are left feeling isolated and confused. Narcissists find it very easy to convince the rest of the world that they are perfectly sane, and they take great pleasure in calling anyone who challenges their false perception of reality "crazy." This is their favorite word, and they will use it to describe anyone who has a normal emotional reaction to their volatile and unstable behavior. Over time, this becomes a complicated form of psychological torture in which the victim is no longer able to trust their own reality and gets sucked into the false reality of the abuser.

ALCOHOL AND DRUG ABUSE

Narcissists are extremely co-dependent; all aspects of the disorder rely upon the resources of others. The desire they have to be idolized is like a physical addiction, so it only makes sense that they are prone to other types of addiction such as drugs, alcohol, shopping, gambling, and workaholism. The narcissist is no different from any other addict—they gain pleasure from the actions and behaviors that feed their narcissistic supply. When they are not able to get this supply from people, they turn to other sources such as alcohol and drugs. These substances not only provide feelings of pleasure, but they also provide an escape from reality. People with NDP will indulge in substance abuse as a form of escapism when their reality is not supporting their imagined sense of self-importance. Basically, when people are not giving them the attention they feel they deserve. Narcissists see their addictions as a way to disassociate themselves from the inferior people they are surrounded by.

Narcissists also feel that they have some type of super-human ability to control their intake of drugs and alcohol;

and when confronted, they will vehemently deny that they have a problem, possibly even more so than an addict that does not suffer with NPD. In their world, they have full control over the addiction and can give up any time they want to. As far as they are concerned, since in their mind they have superhuman ability, illicit substances do not affect them the way they do everyone else. Narcissists are prone to becoming addicted to drugs and alcohol for the following reasons:

- Narcissists need to be highly stimulated
- It is a self-indulgent and selfish act
- It makes them feel complete
- It provides feelings of well-being and power

Narcissists, alcoholics, and drug addicts are prone to the same emotions. They all have unquenchable needs, and there is often a large gap between grandiosity and reality. For narcissists, that is typically the gap between the false mask that they wear and the harsh reality of their lives. Alcohol and drug abuse are self-medication for people with NPD—it is how they handle the pain that is caused by this gap.

When a narcissist is addicted to substance abuse, it is impossible to treat the addiction without first treating the NPD.

EATING DISORDERS

There is a close relationship between narcissistic tendencies and eating disorders. People who suffer from eating disorders are obsessed with body image. The most common types are anorexia (complete starvation), bulimia (purging and binge eating), and purging (eating small amounts of food and then vomiting). All of which are compulsive and impulsive behaviors. Narcissists are impulsive and reckless and can develop an eating disorder for the same reason they become addicted to drugs and alcohol. They have a desire to wield some type of influence or power over an area of their lives. The International Journal of Eating Disorders published a study and found that out of the eighty-four women with an eating disorder, and the seventy women who did not have eating disorders, there was a significantly higher ratio of women in the eating disorder group who exhibited narcissistic tendencies such as grandiosity and entitlement.

It is not common for people diagnosed with an eating disorder to suffer from full-blown NPD; however, there are high numbers of patients with eating disorders who display narcissistic tendencies. Think about it through the lens of the original story: Narcissus fell in love with an image that was unattainable—himself. This is the same as the person with an eating disorder, they are obsessed with an image they can never obtain.

DESTRUCTIVE RELATIONSHIPS

In the Narcissists world, there is no such thing as a successful relationship. This strong belief is typically the result of some early childhood trauma that resulted in feelings of abandonment, betrayal, or humiliation. To the narcissist, any type of emotional attachment to a person is doomed to failure. That means getting attached to a career, home, or even an idea is in the same league as getting attached to a person. They simply have a disdain to getting attached to anything or anyone. For this reason, the narcissist avoids any type of intimacy; they surround themselves with people who will feed their narcissistic supply but won't make any meaningful friendships or relationships where they experience any form of emotional attachment to a person.

It is virtually impossible to be in a relationship with a narcissist; they live in a bubble where all they can see is their own reflection. You can try as hard as you want to, but whoever the significant other is will never get inside that bubble. This leaves them feeling frustrated, hurt, and alone. Narcissists are unable to develop any sense of pleasure or security. The only thing they will emotionally invest in is that which they can fully control—themselves.

One of the major problems with narcissists is their refusal to change their behavior. No matter what problems they are causing at home or at work, or regardless of how many people are complaining about their behavior, they will refuse to acknowledge it and act as if the only person who has a problem is the one doing the complaining. When it comes to any type of disorder, including addiction, the first step to getting any help is admitting that you have a problem. If the narcissist refuses to admit that they have a problem, they will never be able to get the help that they so desperately need.

CHAPTER 2:

WHAT CAUSES NARCISSISM?

Babies are born selfish—it's natural. Their number one concern is getting their immediate needs met and that's it. They have zero understanding of other people's desires and needs. As they transition into their teenage years, this self-centeredness is still very much a part of their nature as they go through the battle to attain independence.

In order to care and protect themselves, children need to develop a healthy level of self-esteem, at the same time as being able to care about others to stay connected to society and family and avoid dangerous influences. When a child has a healthy level of self-esteem, it is an indication that a child feels that they are worthy and loved within their family and valuable to society. The essence of healthy self-esteem is not feelings of self-centeredness because the individual doesn't feel as if they need to trample on others to get their needs met.

There must be a transformation in childish self-centered behavior in order to experience sound mental health in adulthood. The ability to function effectively in a family, and in society is dependent upon the child's ability to gradually see other people's points of view and to experience empathy. So, an emotionally healthy child should eventually become sincere about the well-being of others. The inability to develop empathy as a child is a red flag that they may be at risk of developing a personality disorder in adulthood, and this includes narcissism.

Preteens don't have the mental capability to be manipulative, which is why mental health professionals are reluctant to diagnose NPD any earlier than the age of 18. However, there are certain behaviors in teenagers that indicate that they might be on their way to developing the condition in adulthood.

- Continuous bullying behaviors such as degrading, threatening, making fun of or scapegoating people, including their parents and other adults
- The desire to win regardless of who gets hurt
- Constant lying, they will lie about the lies they tell, blame others for their lies, refuse to accept accountability by attacking those that report them to their parents
- A high and unnatural sense of self-worth
- Determined to get their needs met over others
- An attitude of extreme entitlement that leads them to act as if they should be treated differently than anyone else, and that regardless of the circumstances, they should get what they want
- Aggressive responses to being wronged, criticized, or upset

- Constantly blaming others when things don't work out the way they want
- Less cooperative and more competitive

The bottom line is that NPD is a result of the family environment that a child was raised in. All children want the attention and the approval of their parents, and they adapt to their surroundings. However, there are some home environments that are so destructive that the only way a child is capable of adapting is to become narcissistic. Here are a few scenarios to illustrate this.

WHEN THE PARENTS ARE NARCISSISTS

More often than not, narcissistic parents are going to raise narcissistic children. As we have discussed, narcissists are very high achievers and they will put the same pressure on their children to achieve. Therefore, they will only reward their children when they come first. In this scenario, one or both of the parents are typically "exhibitionist narcissists," and the rule in the household is *there is no point in trying if you are not going to be the best."*

When you are the main character of the school play, you score the most home runs, or you are first in the race, you are showered with attention and praise. Anything less than the best, you are seen as a disappointment and a disgrace to the family. Each child has to prove that they are special, not once, but time and time again. No matter what you achieve, there is still additional pressure to achieve more. As one woman stated during my research, "When I got all A's on my report card, my dad asked why I didn't get an A+."

Children in such families don't feel secure, they know that one wrong move and the love they received the night before will be withdrawn. It's difficult for them to just enjoy being children. Instead of their parents supporting them to find out what they are the most talented at and encouraging them in those areas, they are only supported if they are high achievers. Their parents are not interested in who their children really are, they are only interested in who they want them to be and the type of behavior that will elevate the family's social status. These parents are only interested in their bragging rights and boasting to their friends and family members about how great their children are.

Children who are raised in such households only feel secure and have a sense of self-worth when they are recognized as the best and most successful. The conditional love they received as children, and the overemphasis of success and social status in the home, leads them to develop a habit of chasing success and believing that this is what brings true happiness. David's life is an example of this.

David was a highly successful man who suffered from NPD. He decided to go to therapy because he knew that something just wasn't quite right. He wasn't passionate about anything; his life looked excellent on paper, but he was empty inside. He had lost himself and he didn't know how; although David was a high achiever, he no longer gained any pleasure from his achievements. He started out enjoying his career and his hobbies, but now he only lives his life to impress other people because he gets nothing out of it.

THE NARCISSISTIC PARENT WHO DEVALUES THEIR CHILDREN

In this situation the parent or parents are very dominating. They are always putting their children down and devaluing them. The parent gets angry easily, is always irritable, and has high expectations for the child that are very unrealistic. If there is more than one child in the family, the parent will praise one child and put the other down. The "good child" can quickly become the "bad child," and vice versa. Everyone in the family feels insecure, and the majority of their time is spent attempting to pacify the temperamental narcissistic parent.

If only one of the parents is narcissistic, the other one experiences the same fate as the children. They are belittled and devalued when they don't agree with the narcissistic parent. Children who are brought up in such households feel inadequate, humiliated, and angry and will react to their upbringing in a number of different ways.

The Defeated Child: These children give up on life and accept the labels that have been ascribed to them. During their teenage years, they end up becoming depressed and riddled with self-hate. To numb themselves of the shame they feel, they indulge in addictive behaviors such as drug or alcohol abuse, or they get addicted to the internet.

They find it difficult to achieve anything in life because their childhood years were spent being told that they were worthless.

The Rebellious Child: The rebellious child will reject what they have been told by their parents and spend their lives trying to prove to the world, and especially to their parents that they are not the losers they were referred to as children. They become overachievers and they spend their lives trying to prove that they are special. However, no matter how successful they become, there is always that still small voice criticizing them for every mistake they make.

The Angry Child: They become extremely angry with their parents and the world. Anyone who even slightly resembles their parents becomes the target of their rage. These children are more likely to grow up and become malignant or toxic narcissists where achieving isn't enough, they have to be destructive as well.

We find an example of this type of narcissism in the film *Pretty Woman*. The actor Richard Gere plays a successful businessman who buys companies and then breaks them up. He has a love for destroying the hard work of the former owners because to him, they represent the father that he hated. After hiring a prostitute (Julia Roberts), he eventually falls in love with her and settles down. Even his choice of a love interest is narcissistic. Narcissists have a tendency to want to rescue people, and narcissistic men will only date women they feel they can save, or who are of a lower social standing than them.

The Golden Child: You will find that such parents are closet narcissists who don't enjoy being in the spotlight. To compensate, they put their children in the spotlight instead. The majority of the time the child is extremely talented and deserves the praise and adoration they get. However, the parents will often take it too far and idealize the child. This can lead to the child developing narcissistic tendencies later on in life.

UNCONDITIONAL VERSUS CONDITIONAL LOVE – THE EFFECTS

Everyone wants to be loved unconditionally for who they are. If children feel that their parents only love and value them because they are special, this can lead to insecurity. It is impossible to win all the time, there is always going to be someone else out there who is better than you in some way. Children whose parents idealize them end up believing that they are only worthy when they are being idealized, if not they feel as if they have failed at life.

How They Perceive Flaws and Shame: Children who are idealized become ashamed when they realize that they are not the perfect people their parents raised them to believe they were. They can't handle the fact that they have flaws like everyone else and so strive to be perfect in every area of their lives.

Unable to Identify Who They Really Are: These children are unable to get in touch with who they really are.

They only focus on doing the things that will appease their parents and win their approval. They never spend any time exploring their true identity and discovering what their interests are and where their talents lie.

Occasionally, the golden child may resist their role and avoid becoming narcissistic. They actually feel embarrassed by the over the top praise they receive. The role that has been ascribed to them becomes somewhat of a burden. For example, one child of an overbearing excessive parent told his mother that he no longer wished to be a part of the circus and that he would like to live his life without having to live up to the expectations of his overachieving parents.

THE EXHIBITIONIST ADMIRER

The exhibitionist narcissist parent will reward their children with attention and praise as long as they remain subservient to and admire the parent. These children are trained how to be narcissistic, but at the same time, they are prohibited from being in the limelight. The role they play within the family is to worship the awesomeness of the narcissistic parent without ever being critical of them or trying to surpass them in greatness.

This is how closet or covert narcissists come about, the children learn that they are provided with the narcissistic supplies of praise and attention if they refrain from competing with their narcissistic parents. If they ever attempt to be openly acknowledged as special, these supplies are withheld. The value they are given is based on their ability to act as a crutch to the egotistical nature of the exhibitionist parent.

As adults, children who were raised in these families feel too vulnerable, exposed, and uncomfortable to be in the spotlight, so their self-esteem and narcissism issues are not as obvious to anyone who isn't close to them. Some take on the role and play it very well, ending up in a job supporting an overachieving exhibitionist narcissist that they have nothing but admiration for.

Catherine worked as a personal assistant for the CEO of a successful organization. She had total admiration for him, and her entire life revolved around serving him. Because of her association with such a high-status individual, she felt special, and she lived for any amount of attention and praise she received from him. Catherine kept every birthday and holiday card he had ever given her. Catherine was so in love with her job, as well as having narcissistic tendencies herself, that she never got married. Whenever she met a man who was interested in her, she would compare him to her boss and discount him as unworthy. After working with such a high-profile individual, she felt as if other men were too inferior to waste her time with.

THE BOTTOM LINE

If you are ever concerned that the person you have met may have narcissistic tendencies, ask about their childhood and what their parents were like. Once you get a clear picture of their home environment it won't be difficult to work out whether they have narcissistic tendencies or not.

CHAPTER 3

GASLIGHTING – A FORM OF NARCISSIST ABUSE

One of the most harmful forms of emotional abuse is gaslighting. Narcissists love to use this to tear down their victim's self-confidence to the point where they believe that what they are experiencing is something they have made up in their mind. The aim of this type of manipulation is to disorient and confuse the victim so that they relinquish total control to the perpetrator. The more they can get their victim to doubt that what they are going through is real, the easier it becomes for the narcissist to take over the victim's life.

Gaslighting also eliminates the victim's desire and ability to challenge the abuser because every time they do, the narcissist manages to turn the tables on them so that they feel as if they are in the wrong. Eventually, the victim becomes so paralyzed by fear and doubt that they end up doing everything the narcissist wants them to. They end up losing all self-respect and literally become a puppet to their wicked and calculating master. Here are some examples of gaslighting.

Gaslighting in a Relationship

The most common use of gaslighting is when one partner uses it against another in a relationship. From the outside looking in, the relationship looks perfect, and that is the image that the couple will attempt to portray. The narcissist will start the abuse early. They might tell you they were going to do something on Tuesday, but then when you bring it up, they completely deny saying that they said Tuesday, and that is was Wednesday. This seems pretty innocent, maybe you just got your days mixed up. This is just the start of the relationship and you are really into them, so you let it slide. Looking at something like this in isolation may not necessarily mean you are being gaslighted, it could be that you either misheard or that they accidentally said the wrong day. However, if this type of miscommunication starts happening more often, you will need to start asking questions.

As time goes on, you will start to notice more inconsistencies in what they say. You might suggest going to a Chinese restaurant because they once said that Chinese was their favorite food. You will then get the following response, *"I don't think that would be a good idea babe, I can't stand Chinese, but I know a great Italian place we could try."* At this point, you will start to wonder whether you are going deaf, you were speaking to another person, or they suddenly grew an aversion to Chinese food because you know that is what they said! This is the narcissist's way of making you feel guilty that you are not paying attention when they speak.

As the gaslighting intensifies, the abuser will start to make you feel as if you are the one who is backtracking on what you have said. Depending on how long you have been dating, they may or may not bring this to your attention. If they do, the conversation is likely to go something like this:

You: *"My family is really excited you are coming to Christmas dinner, they are really looking forward to meeting you."*

Them: *"I thought we had agreed to wait a while before we meet each other's families?"*

You: *"We just spoke about this two days ago and you said you couldn't wait to meet my family, especially my little sister."*

Them: *"I said that I am looking forward to getting to know your family, but I also mentioned that I would like to wait another couple of months. You said you thought that was a good idea because you didn't want to rush things, but since you've gone and told them I'm coming, I better come because I don't want to embarrass you."*

By agreeing to come, they are trying to get you to think that they are accommodating you for the mistake that you made (even though you know you didn't make a mistake). Something else the narcissist will do is to respond to your questions or statements with a lie:

"I bought those shoes we spoke about the other day. Remember, you said I could borrow your credit card? I've just ordered them off Amazon."

In this example, they will make up a conversation that you never had, claiming that you said that they could have access to your finances when they needed to. They know that this conversation didn't take place, you know that this conversation didn't take place, but if you attempt to confront them about it, they will lie even more stating that they asked you when you were busy cleaning and you probably don't remember. This is the narcissist's way of getting you to doubt yourself so that they can take total control over your life.

When they can see that they are breaking you down, the narcissist will graduate from subtle deception to full-blown lies, they will start telling you that you did or didn't do something, or that you did or didn't say something. Maybe after asking if they were hungry, they said no and so you put some food in the oven. You go and take a shower expecting your food to be ready when you come out. Instead, you come downstairs to find your partner eating it. They will insist:

> *"I just put this chicken meal in the oven, go and check to see if there is another meal in there because I only saw one when I put this in there. Maybe you heard me turning on the oven and got mixed up that you were doing it."*

As fictitious as this sounds, it works because, in your innocence, you refuse to believe that someone is capable of making up such bold-faced lies. Every time it happens, your self-worth is diminished even further, and you start to question everything you tell yourself.

GASLIGHTING IN THE FAMILY

In a family setting, gaslighting will most likely take place between the parents and the children, with the parents being the perpetrators. Children are extremely vulnerable to this type of manipulation because they rely on their parents for guidance and direction in life. The child is often the recipient of aggressive behavior whether they have done something wrong or not. A typical scenario might involve the following.

School starts at 9 am but it's 9:10 am and no one has left the house yet. The child is too young to leave the house alone and so they are waiting on their parents. The parent will insist that the child is at fault.

"You are late for school now because of your constant messing around, why can't you just learn to behave yourself?"

It is normal for a child to get into trouble because they were playing about and ended up being late for school. However, if the child has done nothing wrong but they are constantly getting blamed for something that they haven't done, it teaches the child that they are just a bad child. This leads to insecurity, low-self esteem, and them living up to the image that their parents have painted of them. It is natural for children to push the boundaries that have been set by them by authority figures. They will do this with their parents and teachers; it is an important process that teaches children about accountability and self-control. Healthy parents will enforce reasonable limits, but some parents are so strict that the slightest indiscretion leads to severe punishment, or they will say things like:

"You are so badly behaved, I really don't know how to cope with you."

Saying things like this reinforces the belief that the child is not good enough and they can't do anything right. It also creates an unhealthy fear in the child and restricts their ability or desire to want to discover and explore who they are. Their own parents have labeled them, and the child now believes that this label is true.

When children are still getting to know themselves and understand their emotions, gaslighting can sow seeds of doubt and make them question whether their feelings are legitimate. In another scenario, the family cat may have died, and the child is crying openly because he is deeply hurt about the loss of the pet. Instead of comforting the child, the parent dismisses his feelings and says: *"I don't know what all those tears are for, you didn't even love the cat anyway. You are just pretending so you can get attention. Your behavior is appalling. I'm the only one who is really upset about this, not you."*

The gaslighting will change as the child turns into a young adult and then an adult. By this stage, they may have become aware that things in the home are not normal and that they are being manipulated. The parent or parents will adapt to the growth stages of the child. One way they might do this is to move away from outright denial that something was said or done and insist that things have been misunderstood or taken out of context. They will then begin to say things like:

> *"You have completely misunderstood what I was trying to say. That's not what I meant at all."*

> *"Your story does sound very similar to what I said, but you've got it totally mixed up."*

Ultimately, statements like this make the child believe that they have taken what their parents have said out of context and that they've got it wrong because of the way they have interpreted the conversation.

Romantic partners and friends will come and go throughout a child's life, but they will still attach importance to these relationships. Even though the parents can see that the child has developed an attachment to these people, they will try to undermine the relationships. The parents will use gaslighting to convince their children that their partners or friends don't really like them, and they will say things like:

> *"You know your friends are only using you because you've got a car, they don't really like you."*

> *"Jason doesn't have true feelings for you, he's only settling because there's no one else at the moment. As soon as someone better comes along, he will leave you."*

"Sandra told me that your friends only invite you out because they know that no one likes you and they feel sorry for you."

"Justin treats you like trash, why do you stand for such behavior, you need to get rid of him."

The child will then start to question whether what their parents are saying is true. Even though they know that their parent is a liar and a manipulator, they will find it difficult not to let these comments affect them. These seeds of doubt that have been planted could potentially destroy a relationship that means a lot to the child.

Earlier you read about how memories are used as a way of confusing someone in a romantic relationship, this is no difference in a relationship between a parent and a child. The only difference is that these memories are not preserved as well because the child was young when the incident took place. A narcissistic parent can take advantage of this situation and tell the child that the event didn't happen the way they think it did, and then twist the facts to their advantage. For example, the sibling might have gotten into trouble at school for being rude to a teacher, but the parent will switch it and say:

"You were such a terrible child when you were younger, I really suffered raising you. Remember when you screamed at Miss Hollingworth and the principal called me to the school? You made me so ashamed!"

The child might be confident that it wasn't them that got into trouble but because it was so long ago, there is a possibility that they might be wrong. If the child attempts to insist that it wasn't them and that it was, in fact, their brother or sister, the parent will swiftly tell them that they are wrong and remind them of how young they were at the time, so they couldn't possibly remember.

When the child becomes an adult, the narcissistic parent will use gaslighting in defense of their parenting skills, they will attempt to convince the child that they had the best upbringing possible.

Child: *"You hit me a lot when I was growing up."*

Parent: *"That's a lie, the only time I ever put my hand on you was when you were really bad and that wasn't often."*

Child: *"I remember differently."*

Parent: *"Well there is something wrong with your memory because you and your brother had the best upbringing. We used to go on vacation all the time, don't you remember?"*

Although these examples are of a parent and child relationship, gaslighting in a family can happen in any context. It can happen between siblings, aunts, uncles, cousins, grandparents, etc.

GASLIGHTING AT WORK

Whether you are dealing with a narcissistic colleague or boss, gaslighting at the workplace does happen. It is typically used as a tactic to maintain or to gain power, and it can drive you insane if you allow it to. Gaslighting at the workplace can take place in one or more of the following ways:

Your boss asks you to do something in the office, you agree to do it and complete the task. After reporting back to your boss to tell him you have finished the job, you are told:

> *"Didn't I tell you to do X? You have gone and wasted the whole day doing something that's totally insignificant to the project we are working on."*

You are not stupid, and you know what you heard, so you get a little bit irate and try and explain that he is mistaken. You are then met with the following comment:

> *"Calm down, don't you think you are taking this a bit out of hand?"*

Another scenario might be, your boss promised you a pay rise after six months, so you've spent the last six months working as hard as you can. You turn up to work before everyone else and leave later than everyone else. Sometimes you come in on weekends when your boss asks you to. So, you are in the seventh month and you decide to jog your boss' memory about the pay raise:

> *"I categorically didn't say you'd definitely be getting a raise. What I did say was that it was something I would consider based on your performance; and so far, I'm not impressed."*

On the other hand, you have a colleague who will do any-thing to get a promotion before you. They will say some nasty things part way through a conversation just to knock your confidence and undermine your ability to get a higher position in the job:

> *"I hear that you might be in a bit of trouble, mate? The boss is fuming about the report you submitted; apparently, it's a load of rubbish! He says he wishes he gave it to me to write instead."*

> *"Didn't you get the email about xyz? Oh, I better not say anything then, you were probably kept out of it because the boss doesn't trust you with such sensitive information yet."*

> *"Oh my goodness, you really need to calm down, I only said you need to put a bit more effort into the job. Gosh, someone woke up on the wrong side of the bed this morning!"*

Additionally, narcissistic and manipulative employees might erase all the information off your hard drive when you go out to lunch. Or move things around when you know you left them in a certain location.

Remember, the main aim of gaslighting is to make you feel insecure and to confuse you. There are several different ways that this can happen.

THEIR SECRET WEAPON

In some cases, the narcissist will intensify the confusion by spending a certain period of time being evil. They will lit-erally have the individual on the brink of walking out the door, then they will do a full 180 and become the kindest, most loving, and charming person ever. The aim of this is to keep the victim hoping that whatever happens, there is always going to be a positive outcome. They then start to believe that the relationship is not that bad after all and they can cope for another day. The side effect of this treatment is that additional seeds of uncertainty are sown into the mind of the victim. Up until this point, the victim has known what to expect, but now, they are not sure what side of the abuser they will see on any given day. This element is especially common in romantic relationships. The victim has such a warped concept of love that they are held in perpetual bondage to their abusive partner.

Additional Signs to Confirm You are Being Gaslighted

The examples listed above might sound familiar to you. If that is the case, this extreme mind manipulation will have had a negative effect on your mental health. If you suspect that you might be a victim of gaslighting, here are some signs that you can identify within yourself that this is the case:

You Have Low Self Esteem

Your opinion of yourself is so low that you accept abusive treatment from your partner. Any confidence you once had in your abilities has been completely diminished, and you believe you deserve what is happening to you. These feelings of low self-worth lead you to turn down opportunities to progress in your career, to socialize, and to grow as a person. There is also the possibility that you experience anxiety because you feel as if you are unable to cope with small challenges.

Your Character Flaws are Your Main Focus

The main aim of a narcissist using gaslighting tactics is to make you feel as if you are not good enough and that you will never be good enough. You will find that you spend copious amounts of time focusing on the things you think are negative about you. In most cases, these will be personality traits that your abusive partner has highlighted. You will start to believe that you are inherently damaged or bad and that your flaws make you unlovable or unlikeable. A narcissist will do this so that you will feel that there is no point in leaving because no one else will want you.

You are Always Questioning Yourself

Did you put the butter in the bread bin and the bread in the fridge by accident? You better go and check just in case. The confidence in your memory has been completely shattered to the point where you find it difficult to function and always feel as if you have done something wrong. The narcissist is happy when they see you acting in this way, it means that you are easier to manipulate, they have managed to convince you that you are crazy, they can deny anything and make up lies and you will believe them.

You Find it Difficult to Make Decisions

You have become incapable of making even the smallest decisions alone. You don't have any confidence in your ability to make the right choices, so in most cases, you will turn to your abusive partner for help. This is a strategic move on their part, they have placed themselves in a position to make you believe that they are the solution to your problems. Again, there is less chance of you leaving if you feel that you need your partner to help you make basic decisions.

You Don't Feel Like Yourself Anymore

You feel as if there is someone else inhabiting your body, you have vague memories of the person you once were, and you are unable to recognize yourself. In a way, you feel as if you are looking back at a past life you once lived.

You Feel Like a Failure

Your self-esteem is so low that you feel like a failure, and you think that everyone else thinks you are a failure too. In your mind, you feel as if there is nothing good about you and that you are incapable of achieving anything in life.

You Are Constantly Apologizing

You feel that if there is a problem, it must be because of you. Regardless of whose fault it actually is, you always feel the need to apologize. This is exactly what the narcissist wants, it means that they will never have to take responsibility for their actions because you will always take the blame.

You Make Excuses for the Narcissist's Behavior

Sometimes your narcissist partner will slip up and treat you badly in front of friends or loved ones. Instead of chastising them, you are quick to defend their behavior and make excuses for them. In your mind they have every right to behave like that, you deserve to be treated in this way.

You Think You are Overreacting

One of the character flaws you see in yourself is that you are oversensitive. You believe that the only reason your partner gets so angry with you is because you overreact to the smallest thing. You think that if you could learn not to get so offended, things would be better for you.

You Avoid Confrontation by Lying to Yourself and Others

You hate confrontation because your partner always manages to defeat you and convince you that you are the one in the wrong. So, in order to avoid the most minor disagreements, you find yourself lying. Instead of saying no to things that are of no benefit in your life, you say yes. You don't question people when they make unreasonable demands from you. For the sake of maintaining peace, you will even act against your own morals and values.

Deep Down You Know Something is Wrong

Somewhere deep in your gut, you know that the relationship you are in is not right. The problem is that you have been blinded to red flags that would be clear to someone who hasn't had their mind manipulated. You are so confused that you can't work out what the issues are and so you are unsure of how to approach them. You always have the thought in the back of your mind that you are the person responsible for the mess you are in.

You Feel Nervous Around the Narcissist

Your entire body tenses up whenever the narcissist walks into the room. This is how the psychological and emotional abuse that you have endured manifests whenever you are in their presence. It is your body's way of preparing for further abuse.

You Can't See Any Way Out

Because of everything you are experiencing, you have resigned yourself to your fate. You don't think there is anything you can do to get out of your situation.

CHAPTER 4

WHAT TO DO WHEN YOUR PARENT IS A NARCISSIST

A narcissistic parent is one who is described as living their lives through their children, overly possessive, or they marginalize their children and compete with them. In general, the narcissistic parent is threatened by their child's independence, even in adulthood. They force their children to live in their shadow, placing unrealistic expectations on them. Parents of narcissistic children are unable to love their children for who they are.

The majority of parents want to be proud of their children, they desire to show them off, they expect them to do well in school, and will be firm when they are displaying destructive behaviors. These are not traits that characterize pathological narcissism. However, the main characteristic of a narcissistic parent is a tendency to deny their children the right to become independent, even in adulthood. The parents believe that the sole purpose of the children is to serve their needs. If you suspect that one or both of your parents are narcissists, here are some signs that your suspicions are correct.

Marginalization: Despite the narcissist's inflated ego, in general, they are extremely insecure people and have a tendency to feel threatened by anyone who has the potential to steal their shine, including their own children. The result of this is that the narcissistic parent will do everything in their power to put the child down so that the parent can maintain their status of perceived superiority. They will do things like compare their children unfavorably to others, nit-pick, criticize and judge them unreasonably, and reject their accomplishments and success. They will say things like, *"You will never be good enough,"* or *"You've always got issues."* By lowering the child's self-esteem, the parent elevates their own self-worth.

During therapy, one girl stated that she begged her mom for money to pay for the lab fee for a science class in college. She agreed to pay for it but reminded her that because she was spending the money on her, she may as well have been burning it.

Lives Through or Uses the Children: The majority of parents want their children to be successful; however, the difference between a narcissistic parent and a normal parent is that they want the child to succeed for their own benefit, so they can say *"Look at what my child has achieved."* Such parents fail to nurture the goals, emotions, and thoughts of the child. The child becomes an extension of the parent's personal desires and is not allowed to become his or her own person.

"Even though I was a tomboy, and I hated dressing up like a girl, my mum used to make me wear these cute frilly dresses. I

think she felt that when people complimented me, it made her look good and boosted her self-esteem."

NARCISSISTIC PARENTS WILL MAKE COMMENTS SUCH AS:

"My son better play for the NBA when he grows up or I'll kill him!"

"Oh, you are such a beautiful little girl, you are going to grow up to be just as stunning as your mother."

"I never had the opportunities that you had when I was growing up, so until you become a lawyer, you are going to do what I tell you."

Superiority and Grandiosity: Most narcissistic parents have an inaccurate inflated self-image. They don't treat people like human beings but as tools used for personal gain. Children of narcissistic parents are treated in the same way, or some are taught to feel as if they are superior to others and that people are simply objects to be disposed of once they have been used. This grandiose sense of entitlement is achieved by diminishing humanity.

Manipulation: Narcissistic parents who manipulate their children often do so in one or more of the following ways.

Shaming: *"Your inability to achieve is a disgrace to the family."*

Blaming: *"I wish you were never born; you are the reason why I am not happy."*

Guilt trip: *"You are so ungrateful, after everything I've done for you in this world."*

Unreasonable Pressure: *"You WILL get an A and make your parents proud."*

Negative Comparison: *"Why can't you be as clever as your sister?"*

Manipulative Punishment and Reward: *"If you don't go to college to become a doctor, I won't financially support you through your studies."*

Emotional Coercion: *"Unless you are able to meet my expectations, you are not a good child."*

The common thread that runs through this type of manipulation is conditional love. I will only love you if you do this, and I will withdraw my love if you do that. They are incapable of expressing healthy parenting skills.

Superficial Image: Some narcissistic parents enjoy showing the world how amazing their family is. They take great pleasure in publicly parading what they think they have that is superior to others, whether it's physical appearance, material possessions, accomplishments, projects they are a part of, memberships to a specific club, a trophy wife or husband, good looking children, or connections to people in high places. Whatever it is, they do their best to seek flattery and attention. For a lot of narcissistic parents, social media is a dream come true, as it gives them the opportunity to post pictures of their supposedly perfect lives with the underlying message being *"My life is so wonderful, look what I've achieved!"*

"The image that my mother displays in public is nothing like the person she really is."

Touchy and Inflexible: Some narcissistic parents are very rigid when it comes to how they expect their children to behave. Every minor detail is regulated, and when the child steps outside of those boundaries, all hell breaks loose. There are many different reasons a narcissistic parent will become irritated with their child. It may be because they are not paying enough attention, they are not doing what they have been asked, or the parent may feel as if they fall short in certain areas. It can even be as simple as being in the parent's presence at the wrong time. One of the reasons for this type of touchy behavior from the parent is a desire to control the child, and when they are not able to control the child's every move, the parent reacts in rage.

"I can't stand it when you arrange the cans in the cupboard that way, I have told you before I HATE IT."

Dependency/Co-dependency: There are some narcissistic parents who expect their children to take care of them for the rest of their lives, whether it is physically, financially, or emotionally. Although there is nothing wrong with looking after your parents, especially when they get older, the problem is when the narcissistic parent manipulates their children into doing so and makes unreasonable demands on them with total disregard to the needs of their children.

"My mom is a single parent; she demands that I take care of her financially or she won't be able to survive."

Possessiveness and Jealousy: Narcissistic parents hope that their children will always live under their influence. When the child begins to mature and become independent, the parent becomes exceptionally jealous and possessive. This independence can take the form of making their own friends to choosing their own academic or career path. Such behavior is interpreted negatively and taken personally. In particular, a romantic partner becomes a huge threat to the parent, so they often respond with criticism, rejection, and competition. The narcissistic parent doesn't believe that any partner, no matter how well they treat their child is good enough.

"How dare that man take my daughter away from me! Who does he think he is?"

Neglect: There are some narcissistic parents who just leave their children to get on with it. Their main concern is themselves and they are too self-absorbed to care about what their children are doing. Whatever activities they are participating in provides the narcissist parent with the stimulation, validation, and feelings of self-importance that they crave. This could be in the form of hobbies, a career, personal adventures, or social flamboyance.

> *"My husband is never at home, he is basically an absent father, he is always off doing something that he enjoys rather than spending time with our child. He is a very selfish individual."*

One of the most common characteristics of a narcissistic parent is a lack of empathy. The parent has no consideration for the child's thoughts and feelings, and the only thing that's important to the parent is how they think and feel. Children who are raised in this type of environment will do one of several things to survive. They will either stand up for themselves and fight back, they will distance themselves, or some will develop a false persona to deal with the pain of who their parents have caused them to be. In this way, they are developing narcissistic characteristics.

MY PARENT(S) ARE NARCISSISTS – NOW WHAT?

So, you've worked out that one or both of your parents are either full-fledged narcissists or they have narcissistic tendencies. Regardless of the situation, you have a right to live a normal and healthy life no matter what your parents are doing. You may feel as if you need to help them, but the truth is, it's not your responsibility. Even if you are still living under your parents' roof, there are several ways you can help yourself.

Learn About the Condition: The more you know about narcissism, the easier it will be for you to navigate your situation. There are plenty of books and resources on the internet that will give you more information about the condition.

Accept That Your Narcissistic Parent Might Never Change: One of the main character traits of a narcissist is that they refuse to accept responsibility for their actions. They will never admit that they are wrong and as you have read live in their own little world of self-importance. As much as you love your parents and you would like them to change, this is not something you can encourage them to do. A lot of children of narcissistic parents hope that their parents will one day love them for who they are. Unfortunately, unless your mother or father accepts that they have a problem, which may never happen, they will never get the help that they need, and you will never experience the love that you have craved your entire life.

Recognize That One of Your Parents is an Enabler: If one of your parents is a narcissist, the other parent is the enabler. Enablers excuse the behavior of the narcissist, which leads to normalizing and sustaining the behavior. Sometimes the enabler also assists their narcissist in their exploits by perpetuating and condoning the abuse. The enabler is often a victim of the abuse, but by refusing to call it out when it's happening to the child, the other parent is indirectly participating in the abuse.

Sometimes it is even more difficult to forgive the enabling parent than the narcissistic parent. This is because you know that the enabler is sane, and they really don't have any excuse for not protecting you. This can lead to terrible feelings of betrayal.

Understand the Family Roles: What is the role you play in the family, are you the golden child? Have you ever been the enabler? In a narcissistic family, the roles are often fluid, but this depends on the agenda of the narcissist. You may have been the golden child and the angry child because the narcissist controls the family by utilizing the divide and conquer strategy. As a result, you may feel alienated from your siblings (if you have any), and from your other parent. There is also the possibility that you feel as if they have betrayed you. However you might be feeling, it is important to remember that all family members are a part of a twisted system that has been constructed by the dominant narcissist in the house with the sole purpose of serving their needs to the detriment of others. Each one of you has had to fight to survive after being forced into your perspective roles.

A united front is the most powerful defense against the narcissist. If you are on one accord with the rest of the family members, this is the easiest way to put an end to narcissist abuse. However, if this is not the case, your next course of action is to defend yourself against the narcissistic parent.

Set Boundaries: This will infuriate the narcissist, but you have to be strong and continue to enforce them. Narcissists enjoy violating boundaries; they believe that they own their children and it is their right to control and manipulate them. If you are the golden child, your job is to live the way your parent wishes they could have lived, and then project this false image to the world. Regardless of your role, the child of a narcissist is objectified and their identity as a person is ignored. The narcissist decides how you are supposed to think and feel and demands that you comply with their version of reality. If you don't, you will have to suffer the consequences. One of the hardest things you will have to do is establish healthy boundaries.

Get in Touch with Your Feelings: Children of narcissistic parents have been indirectly trained to deny their feelings. In the house, they are not important and the only person that matters is the narcissistic parent. Your feelings are threatening to the narcissist because more than likely, they are going to conflict with the needs, demands, and beliefs of the narcissistic parent. Your feelings are denied through shame, ridicule, rage, and other forms of attack, which lead you to hate or even fear your feelings. One of the most important things you can do for yourself as a victim of narcissist abuse is to reconnect with your feelings. You may feel as if you don't have any because you have had to suppress them for so many years, but they are there. Allow yourself to feel your emotions, treat them with respect. You will find yourself in your feelings and maneuverer your way out of the web of splendor that you had been entrapped by. Your parent(s) have violated you and hurt you in the worst possible ways, and you will have to work your way through these feelings of extreme pain and anger. The majority of narcissists project their inability to feel any emotions onto others, they will even go as far as accusing them of the same abusive behavior they are displaying. So, when you first start this process, you will find it difficult to differentiate between your own feelings and the ones you have been brainwashed to believe. Be patient with yourself as you learn to reconnect with your feelings again.

Stop Harming Yourself: People raised in narcissistic families are prone to self-abuse. Since they have been indirectly trained to hate themselves, they are prone to indulge in self-punishing, self-destructive, and thrill-seeking behaviors such as substance abuse. If you fall into this category, you are internalizing the abuse you were exposed to. By harming yourself in this way, you are allowing your narcissistic parent to yield the same power over you as they did when you were a child. You will also make the psychological and emotional trauma you were forced to endure worse. Patterns of addiction and self-harm can be difficult to break, so it is important that you get professional help to assist you with this.

Be Aware of Your Attraction to Narcissists: To add insult to injury, children who experienced narcissist abuse grow up to attract narcissists as partners, friends, and managers. This is not a nice thing to have to deal with; however, if you have fallen victim to narcissist abuse in adulthood, you simply have to learn from your mistakes and move forward. This is one of the main reasons it's important to educate yourself about narcissism. It will help you to develop a high-powered radar against narcissists so that you can protect yourself against them.

Accept How You Feel About Your Narcissist Parent: All children love their parents, in most cases, regardless of what they do. They want love, adoration, and attention from their parents. Unfortunately, the narcissistic parent is incapable of loving their children the way they deserve to be loved. Combined with anger and grief, you may also feel sorry for your parent. There is also the possibility that you have no feelings for your parent because you have been too abused to love anymore.

Regardless of how you feel, try not to be too harsh on yourself for it, acknowledge your feelings and allow them to guide you in the way you interact with your family. If you feel like the safest choice is to break contact with them, then that is what you should do. Or be strict with your boundaries and lower your expectations. Unless narcissist parents are totally sadistic, some of them are capable of showing their children affection, even if it doesn't really come from the heart. It may not be often, but they will do so sometimes, so when it's there, take it.

Cleanse Yourself of Narcissistic Fleas: When you are raised by narcissistic parents, there is a high possibility that you are going to pick up some of their traits. These are referred to as "narcissistic fleas," and nobody wants fleas, and you definitely don't want to end up like your narcissistic parent(s)! The good news is that you can avoid this if you are aware and mindful of your situation. The fact that you have already come to the realization that your parent(s) is a narcissist is a good starting point. Now it is your responsibility to ensure that you don't take on the same characteristics. Examine yourself thoroughly, what are your triggers? Is there anything you do that reminds you of your narcissistic mother or father? Do you have a bad temper? Do you use manipulation or guilt to gain control and seek attention? Are you sensitive to the needs and perspectives of others?

We don't have any choice in how we were raised, but we can choose how we react to it. Being brought up in a narcissistic household is very traumatic and no child should have to live with that. Unfortunately, we can't choose who our parents are, we simply have to make the most of what we have. The best revenge in life is success, so instead of allowing your bad upbringing to destroy you, allow your pain to propel you into your purpose in life.

CHAPTER 5:

EMPATHS AND NARCISSISTS – THE TOXIC COUPLE

Opposites attract is a statement that most people have heard all their lives. While this saying has the potential to get you to step outside of your comfort zone and interact with people that you normally wouldn't, it can also be pretty dangerous.

As you have read, narcissists are attracted to people they can use; and empaths are often their main targets. Empaths and narcissists are complete opposites. Narcissists don't have any empathy and live for admiration. Empaths, on the other hand, are in tune with other people's emotions and are extremely sensitive. They are like emotional sponges and absorb the energy of the people around them. These character traits appeal to narcissists because they see empaths as people who will selflessly cater to their needs.

A Train Wreck Waiting to Happen

A relationship between an empath and a narcissist will never work out. Narcissists are attracted to empaths because they see them as loving, giving people who are going to be totally devoted to them. Empaths are attracted to narcissists because of the false image that they portray; they appear to be extremely charming, giving, and intelligent until you don't do what they say and their true cold nature comes out. When a narcissist wants to hook someone, they will be attentive and loving, but that mask will soon disappear. At the start of the relationship, they only see the good side of the narcissist, sparks will fly, and the empath will feel as if they have found the love of their life. This doesn't last very long because narcissists are full of hatred and they believe that everyone is beneath them. Once the narcissist starts to notice that the empath has flaws, they stop idealizing them and start victimizing them for not being perfect. Not only that, but they begin to resent the empath's natural ability to empathize with people. They start getting frustrated and lashing out at the empath for being too dramatic or sensitive. Suddenly, their emotions are no longer an asset but a flaw.

What makes a narcissist turn so quickly? The narcissist loves being admired, and once he's got everything he needs, he no longer has a need for the empath and starts to pull away. But the empath won't leave, they will wait around for the narcissist to need them again and the cycle continues. It is difficult for an empath not to fall in love with a narcissist because it goes against their instincts. They believe that they can fix people and heal them with compassion. Empaths find it difficult to believe that a person is incapable of showing empathy.

NARCISSISTS LOVE CHAOS AND DRAMA

Empaths will do anything for peace and harmony, whereas narcissists love chaos and drama and enjoy pulling people's strings. They enjoy manipulating empaths by leading them on with intermittent hope. They will incorporate kindness and compliments into their behavior and lead the empath to believe that if they behave in the right way, they will get the kind and loving person back that they first met. Empaths believe that all humans make mistakes and so they are willing to be patient with people they think are struggling with personal development. If a narcissist tells an empath that they want to change, an empath will stick around waiting for it to happen. Narcissists have a strategy they use where they will admit that they've got issues, but they don't follow through with making changes. This is how they reel the empath back in, and it works with them because they want to help their partner grow and support them. Because empaths are naturally caretakers, they can sense that the narcissist has an underlying problem and they desperately want to fix it. However, what they are unable to see is that the narcissist lives to take from people, and they will feed off them like an energy vampire. The more attention the narcissist is given, the more victimized and drained the empath will become.

WHEN THE RELATIONSHIP BECOMES TOXIC

The narcissist is driven by ego—they live for the love and attention shown to them by the empath. After a while, they realize that they get more attention from the empath when she is in the narcissist's bad books. At this point, they will begin to manipulate and engineer situations, and it is at this stage that the relationship starts to become emotionally abusive. The narcissist will introduce an element of control to enable him to dominate the relationship. They will start casually dropping demeaning and destructive comments so that the empath doesn't step out of line. Sensitive people can't handle being told they are not good enough, so they start thinking that if they try harder or love them a bit more things will go back to normal. Unfortunately for the empath, that's exactly what the narcissist wants. They want you to keep giving more, but your more will never be enough— EVER! The narcissist will keep taking, and the empath will keep giving until they don't have anything left to give.

At this point, one of two things will happen: The empath will get so emotionally drained that they can no longer provide narcissistic supply, and the narcissist then gets bored and leaves the relationship because she is no longer feeding him. Or the empath will get an epiphany, realize what's going on and leave. Either way, the relationship is destined for failure—it will never work and there is no point in trying to force it.

EMPATHS AND TRAUMA BONDING

Empaths will typically form a trauma bond with their narcissistic partner. The push and pull nature of the relationship leads to the victim feeling as if it's impossible to leave the relationship, no matter how much damage is being caused. Narcissists take advantage of the empath's willingness to look at themselves and acknowledge their faults, which becomes a vicious cycle for the empath. Due to the intuitive nature of the empath, they can typically sense that their partner is a narcissist and that they are not really capable of having a genuine love for them. However, due to the abusive nature of the relationship, it becomes extremely difficult to break free from the cycle of destruction and attraction. Anytime she is hurt for whatever reason, the empath becomes isolated because the narcissist is unable to comfort her.

It Will Not Get Better

It is essential that the empath understands that the narcissist is so wounded, there is nothing she can do to fix him. The relationship is never going to get better, it is only going to get worse. The empath does not have the ability to empathize and must exit the relationship before her self-esteem and energy are worn down any further. Since the narcissist doesn't have any empathy and the relationship benefits him because of the ample narcissistic supply he is receiving, he will never put an end to the relationship. Therefore, the empath must find the strength to get out quickly before it is too late.

How to Avoid Getting into Another Relationship with a Narcissist

Narcissists are extremely charismatic, and it's difficult not to get caught up in their charm. If you are not aware, it can be difficult to single them out because they are so skilled at camouflaging themselves. They are social chameleons, and they know exactly how to manipulate your feelings with what they say. It is important that sensitive people are aware that they are easy prey for narcissists, but they should never confuse this with being powerless. Here are some tips to assist you in avoiding narcissists.

Know Who You Are: When you know what you stand for and what you will and won't accept, the narcissist, or any other person for that matter, will have a difficult time convincing you that you don't deserve to be in a healthy relationship. Having the ability to tune into the emotions of others is a powerful gift, it is something that makes you an awesome and amazing person. However, spend some time alone and tune into your own feelings to get an idea of who the person pursuing you really is.

Recognize the Red Flags: As mentioned, narcissists know how to hide who they really are. However, they will reveal themselves if you look hard enough. Empaths have a habit of ignoring people's bad characteristics because they think every human being is deserving of compassion. However, there are some things that should not be overlooked.

- He's Possessive: You've just met him, but he has a problem with you having friends or wanting to spend time with your family.

- You Never Look Good Enough: At the beginning of a relationship, a narcissist will never directly tell you that you don't look good in what you are wearing. However, he will make suggestions and say things like, "I think you look better in black."

- They Are Rude to Other People: He might be as nice as pie to you because he is trying to reel you in, but he treats everyone else like something off the bottom off his shoe! This is a real indicator of his true character.

- He Speaks Badly about His Ex: Some relationships just don't end well and that's life. However, if he is constantly insulting his ex, and blaming her for everything that went wrong in the relationship, he has got some serious issues.

- He's Controlling: Possessive and controlling are two completely different things. Someone of a controlling nature is going to try to tell you what to wear, what to eat, how to sit, etc. Run away if you get a hint of such behavior.

CHAPTER 6

WHY VICTIMS STAY – EMOTIONAL AND PSYCHOLOGICAL REASONS

Unfortunately, abusive relationships are extremely common; according to statistics, one out of every four women will be abused by a partner at some point in their lives. Abuse is also one of the crimes that goes unreported the most, which means that there are probably more cases of abuse than we are made aware of.

WHAT IS TRAUMATIC BONDING?

The biological process of bonding allows an emotional connection to develop between two people; normally, this is through a positive experience. The word "bonding" is generally associated with positive images of loving and intimate moments being shared by families and couples. The opposite of this is traumatic bonding where a bond is created between two people in an abusive relationship. The average person cannot understand why someone would stay with someone who hurts them, the answer lies in the psychological need to survive. Traumatic experiences cause us to shut ourselves off emotionally; numbness sets in, and in order to survive, our primal instincts kick in. One of the things the abuser does is subconsciously focus on the positive characteristics of the one being abused and ignore the fact that she has just had her two front teeth knocked out by the man who is supposed to love her. How many times have you heard a battered woman talk about the hell she is going through only to state, *"But, he's a really nice guy though."*

Trauma bonding is associated with The Stockholm Syndrome (TSS), a psychological disorder named after a hostage situation that took place in 1973. According to reports, the hostages formed an emotional attachment to their kidnappers. They stated that they were more afraid of the police who rescued them than the perpetrators. They even went as far as to set up a fund to help pay their legal fees!

Trauma bonding takes place through a process of conditioning that psychologists have referred to as the "arousal-jag." This is where the narcissist gives their victim something to make them happy and then takes it away. This is done strategically over and over again, and it is this that creates the trauma bond. The narcissist is connected to the feeling of the excitement that he or she experiences when they do what they do. This is one of the reasons narcissists have more than one partner—the excitement factor is intensified. The victim becomes attached to the chaos, and sadly they eagerly wait for it, and this is an additional bonus for the narcissist.

The narcissist takes their victim through a process of devaluing them—there is a period of neglect and betrayal. Just before they are about to get discarded, the victim feels a sense of loss, and the behavior of the narcissist indicates that they are going to leave. The victim experiences nervousness, fear, and anxiety after the walkout. They get an overwhelming urge to call the narcissist, and at this point, they are thriving off the chaotic feeling that the narcissist has created. The victim becomes addicted to his behaviors, and when he leaves, they miss him, and when the narcissist goes silent, it's absolute torment to the victim. They would rather that he was screaming in their face than saying nothing because at least he is showing some type of emotion and the victim knows where they stand. Despite the fact that the connection between the narcissist and his victim has been manufactured and manipulated, the victim has gotten to a point where they simply can't live without it. After an extended period of absence, the narcissist will turn up just before the victim can do anything stupid. He will reinforce the silent treatment knowing that his victim is just satisfied that she has access to him. The narcissist conditions his victims to keep lowering their standards so that he can get away with doing even more evil.

PSYCHOLOGICAL ABUSE IS ADDICTIVE

What does abuse look like to most people? If this question was put forward to the general public, most would speak of the evil physically abusive characters they see in films and on TV. They beat their partners, scream at them, and even kill them in fits of rage. Although abuse of this nature does take place, it does not provide an accurate representation of the abuse that people in the real-world experience. Therapist Shannon Thomas explains that psychological abuse is like a poison that slowly enters the veins through an IV drip.

It begins with an insult here and a back-handed comment there. The victim will typically brush these incidents off as random events because narcissists are experts at pretending that they are the perfect partner, and as stated, they will shower their partner with love and affection. As the mask begins to slip, the victim convinces herself that the narcissist's behavior is out of character and that they are the ones responsible for making their partner angry. People get trapped in these relationships because they believe that if only they try a little bit harder, they can win back their partner's affection. This cycle leads them to become addicted to the abuse in the same way that the addict becomes addicted to drugs.

A psychologically abusive relationship is like being on an emotional roller coaster. The victim is rewarded with kindness when they "behave" according to the narcissist's standards, but this is often inconsistent. This puts the body through trauma as a combination of cortisol (during punishment) and dopamine (during affection) is released. This causes the body to become biologically addicted to the treatment it is receiving. The victim is desperate for the connection she had with the narcissist at the beginning of the relationship, but what she fails to realize is that the connection was false. The nice side of the narcissist that was used to reel in the victim doesn't exist. After a while, this game of cat and mouse causes the body to become dependent on getting that approval. This hormonal rollercoaster puts a lot of stress on the body, and it manifests physically through conditions such as acne and chest pains, and in very severe cases, autoimmune disorders. The body will begin to shut down and experience arthritic type pains, migraines, chronic pains, and it will become difficult to fight infections.

Despite the stress that their bodies are being put through, victims stay in these relationships because they are unable to see clearly. They have become confused, disillusioned, and disorientated because of the intermittent love, control, and manipulation that the victim has been through. The narcissist has backed them into a corner of desperation and self-blame.

Due to traumatic bonding, if the victim does leave, they will eventually return, and others don't even make an attempt to leave. A relationship with a narcissist will always follow a pattern of idealization, devaluation, and discarding. Since narcissists depend on supply, if the victim becomes so broken that they are no longer capable of providing that supply, they abandon them permanently and move on to the next victim. Sometimes, this is the only way a victim will break free from her abuser, and it is at this point that the victim can come to terms with the fact that they have been in an abusive relationship. They will go through a grieving process in which they realize how damaged they have become and that nothing that happened to them was their fault. This is when healing can take place and the survivor is made aware that they were not targeted because they were weak, but because they had such a giving heart.

Here are signs that you or someone you know might be in a trauma bond:

- Your partner is always promising you things but never delivers
- Your partner does or says something to you around other people that disturbs them, but you brush it off or make excuses for his behavior
- You can't see any way out of the relationship, and you feel stuck
- You have constant arguments with your partner that never get resolved
- You are given the silent treatment or punished by your partner when you do or say something that he doesn't like
- You feel as if you can't detach yourself from your relationship even though deep down you know that something is wrong
- When you do leave the relationship, you feel as if you physically can't cope with being away from him
- You do everything you can to please your partner even though you know you are not getting the same treatment in return
- You desperately try to win his approval although it is obvious he is using you

- You continue to trust in him even though he is perpetually unreliable
- You desperately desire to be understood by your abusive partner even though it's clear he doesn't care
- You are loyal to your partner when he has betrayed you

HOW TO HEAL FROM TRAUMATIC BONDING

Once you get out of an abusive relationship with a narcissist, the healing process is essential for you to move forward in life. Here are some steps to help you.

See a Therapist: Therapy is essential to the healing process, as it will help you see things that you are unable to on your own. What you have been through will have severely damaged your mental health and will take some time to repair. A therapist will help you understand how you ended up in an abusive relationship. They will evaluate your childhood and explain how that contributed to you being attracted to such a person. They will also provide you with coping strategies to deal with the grieving process.

Allow Yourself to Grieve: At the end of the day, even though it's a good thing that you've gotten out of the relationship, you are still going to feel as if you have lost something. Regardless of whether you have been in the relationship for months or years, you are going to be upset that it has come to an end. You gave your heart and soul to a person who took advantage of you and abused you. The individual might not be worth mourning over, but the situation must be mourned so that you can move on with your life. You have experienced the death of a relationship, the death of the illusion that your relationship was under, and you have just come to the conclusion that you have been living a lie. According to grief expert Elisabeth Kubler-Ross, you will go through five stages of grief.

- **Denial:** At this stage, the world becomes overwhelming and meaningless. You can't understand why this had to happen to you, you are in a state of denial and shock. You feel numb inside and don't know how you are going to continue living. You will struggle to find reasons to live. However, shock and denial make it easier for you to cope with what has happened. Denial helps to process the feelings associated with grief. It is nature's way of only allowing in as much as we can handle. As time goes on, you will begin to accept that you have lost this person, and you will start asking yourself questions. This is when the healing process begins. You will start getting stronger, and you will start confronting your feelings instead of denying them.

- **Anger:** Anger is required for proper healing to take place, even though it will feel like it is never going to end. Accept your anger—the more you allow yourself to feel this emotion the less it will have control over you, and you will begin to heal.

You will also experience several other emotions during the stage of anger. They are different for each person, and you will become familiar with them as you go through them. Anger is limitless, and you will take it out on many people including family, friends, therapists, the person you ended the relationship with, and if you are religious, God. You will wonder whether God has abandoned you in all of this. Your anger is covering up the pain that you really feel—it is natural to feel abandoned and deserted. There is strength in anger. It serves as an anchor and provides temporary structure to the empty feeling of loss. In the beginning, grief feels as if you are lost at sea, in the middle of an ocean with nothing to hold onto. When you get angry, structure is formed, the anger allows you to connect to something, it builds a bridge over the endless sea that you feel that you are lost in, and now you have something to hold onto as you try and walk out this stage of grief. Although anger is not a nice feeling, it is better than the denial stage because at least you are feeling something. The anger that you feel is an indication of the intensity of the love that you felt for your partner.

The more you learn to love yourself, the angrier you will become. You will start to feel frustrated at the fact that you allowed someone to treat you in this way. When you start experiencing these emotions, take a drive somewhere, go to the beach or a secluded location and scream and cry, release every negative emotion from your system. Do this as many times as you need to. Never self-harm by cutting yourself, drinking, or taking drugs as a way of numbing the pain. Instead, face your emotions head on. This is the only way you will prevent yourself from becoming a victim. If you want to beat this, harming yourself is not the way to do it.

- **Bargaining:** Bargaining comes in the form of *"what if…."* statements. No matter how destructive your relationship was, you will want it to go back to normal because you can't handle the feeling of that person no longer being in your life. You will want to rewind the hands of time, *"Could I have been a better girlfriend," "What if I could cook better," "What if I cleaned the house better?"* Guilt and bargaining go hand in hand, you will feel as if it was your fault that the relationship broke down and you will think about all the things that you could have done differently to make the relationship work. Since you know that you will never get your partner back, you may even start to bargain about the pain you are feeling, and begin to say things like, *"I would do anything not to feel like this anymore."* It is important to remember that these stages don't have a time limit—they can last for minutes, hours, weeks, or months. They are not stages that you step in and out of in chronological order, you will move back and forth between each of them. After the bargaining stage has ended, you will begin to focus your attention on the present, you will start to feel empty, and the feelings of grief will intensify.

- **Depression:** The feeling of depression will feel as if it will never end. You will feel as if you are stuck in the bottom of a black pit with no way out. Depression does not mean that you are suffering from mental illness, it is a normal stage of the grieving process. You are supposed to feel this way after losing someone that was a significant part of your life. You will feel intense sadness at this stage and wonder if you can continue living life alone. Even though you were in an abusive relationship, losing someone you love is depressing and this is an appropriate and normal response to what you are going through. Not to experience depression would be considered abnormal, and when it finally settles in your soul that you can't fix the relationship, that there is no going back, depression will take over you.

- **Acceptance:** This stage of the grieving process is often misinterpreted as being okay with what has happened, that you have gotten over it and you are moving on with your life. This is far from the truth. The majority of people will never be okay that they have lost someone important in their life and, in particular, that you spent the majority of those years being abused. It is going to take a while for you to get over this. The acceptance stage is about accepting that the relationship is over, you will never return to it, and that you are now living in a new normal. You must now try to live in a world where the person you loved is no longer a part of it. You can no longer pick up the phone and call him when you want, you can't turn up at his house, and he isn't going to be turning up at your house. That chapter of your life is now closed and it's time to move forward. Because of the abuse that you have endured, you may even feel like you are betraying your partner when you move on, especially when you learn how to be happy. When you have spent so much time being told that you don't deserve happiness, you start to believe it, which is part of the reason you stayed in the relationship in the first place. However, you must evolve, grow, and move onto greener pastures. As you start to invest in yourself and relationships with others, you will start living again. However, you will not be able to do so until you have given some time to the grieving process.

This idea is totally optional; however, it is worth mentioning because some abuse victims do report that it brings a sense of closure. You might want to take part in a burial ceremony in which you bury or burn all the belongings of your partner. Things like cards, letters, gifts, and clothes, you can either put them in a box and bury them, or you can burn them in a bonfire and say goodbye to them forever.

Live in the Moment: After an abusive relationship, people tend to focus on what could have been. Even though they are no longer in the relationship, due to the psychological damage that has taken place, they feel that if they had done things differently the relationship may have gone in a different direction. Survivors of psychological abuse fail to understand that what happened had nothing to do with them but everything to do with the abuser. Narcissists seek out people they can abuse, they know what they are doing is wrong, which is why they wear a mask at the beginning stages of the relationship. Therefore, instead of focusing on the past or the future, focus on the present, how you feel right now. Do you feel unloved, trapped, unworthy? Do you feel as if you compromised your morals and values to be in this relationship? Stop waiting and hoping and put your energy into what is taking place now and the effect it is having on you.

Process Your Emotions: When you have just left an abusive relationship, your emotions are going to be severely damaged, so it is important that you take some time out to process what you are feeling. You are going to miss your partner—you will feel alone, depressed, helpless, frustrated, and even angry. It is important that you don't suppress your emotions but recognize them as valid and accept them for what they are. A great way to release your emotions is to join a martial arts class. You will be able to release your pain on a punching bag instead of internalizing it.

Reconnect with Loved Ones: One of the main strategies of a narcissist is to isolate their victims. They will force you to cut ties with friends, family members, and loved ones because they don't want anyone else to influence you but them. If this is something you have experienced, make an effort to reconnect with the people you were once associated with. You will probably feel slightly embarrassed to do this since there may be people you haven't spoken to in months or even years. However, if they are level-headed people, when you explain your situation, they will understand. They will be able to encourage you and support you as you go through the healing process.

If you find this too difficult, look for opportunities to meet new people. A great way to do this is to join a domestic survivor's group. You will meet people exactly like you who have been in similar relationships. You will be able to relate to each other on a deeper level than those who have not experienced psychological abuse.

PROTECTION STRATEGY: HOW TO BREAK FREE FROM A NARCISSIST

You will experience several difficult phases when you are in a relationship with a narcissist. There are going to be times when you feel so abused, humiliated, and alone that all you want to do is give up. You will feel exhausted, worthless, and rejected. You will feel intense pain, but at the same time you will not want to face the reality of the situation, so you will convince yourself that things are okay just so that you can feel better. But in the long run, you will feel much worse as you begin to realize that you were only deceiving yourself. There are times when you will feel as if you are in a prison and there is no escape. This process is going to be challenging, but you must start somewhere. Start by training yourself to become immune to their egocentrism. Here are some steps to do this.

- Be determined and independent, live your life the way you want to.

- Don't allow discussions and arguments to drain your emotions and energy.
- Stop giving the person compliments, attention, and praise—these things are what fuel the narcissist.
- Keep your conversations with the person short. Narcissists enjoy being at the center of attention, and by engaging with them, you are feeding them energy.
- Do not stoop to the same level as the narcissist. As much as they are annoying you and you want to give them a taste of their own medicine, this is not a good idea. The narcissist will enjoy going back and forth with you, and in the end, you will lose. Remember, the narcissist is an experienced player, you are not.

After a while, the narcissist in your life will get fed up with you. They only stick around when they have something to gain, and since you are no longer providing them with narcissistic supply because their behavior and comments don't have an effect on you, they will look elsewhere. Once they find another victim, just know that your name will be dragged through the dirt. They will tell their new partner how terrible you were and how badly you treated them to make their next victim feel sorry for them.

Once they have left, you will go through a grieving period in which you will start to feel pity for the narcissist. You will convince yourself that they are only like this because they are deeply depressed. There is no need to feel this way, everything that the narcissist says or does is calculated and well thought out. They do not act on impulse or from a place of despair. They know exactly what they are doing. The narcissist only starts feeling depressed when they have run out of supply; therefore, they will go out looking for new stimuli (alcohol, drugs, the opposite sex, shopping). Once they get their supply, they are back to their normal selves again. Instead of spending time feeling sorry for yourself, engage in the following to get over this feeling of guilt that you are experiencing.

- Eat well and exercise, take care of your physical body.
- Go for a walk and meet up with people who will make you feel better.
- Talk to people you trust to get it out of your system.
- Cry and shout for as long as you need to.
- Relax by taking a long bath or shower.
- Go to the movies or rent a film—this will take your mind off what is going on in your own life.
- Start journaling—this will help you to get in touch with your emotions and release the ones that are of no benefit to you.
- Buy yourself something nice.
- Become a volunteer—this will show you that there are more important people to take care of than your narcissistic partner.
- Take part in alternative therapies such as Eye Movement Desensitization and Reprocessing

(EMDR) or Emotional Freedom Technique (EFT). They are effective therapies that assist in releasing and overcoming painful emotions.

- Surround yourself with positive people who will give you hope that there is light at the end of the tunnel.
- Get rid of anything in your house that reminds you of your partner.
- If your partner was controlling and only allowed you to wear the clothes that they liked, give those clothes to charity and start wearing clothes that you like.
- The attention that you once gave to your narcissistic partner should now be given to yourself.

Now that you know you are dealing with a narcissist, your next step is to get as far away from them as possible. This is the hard part! As you have read, extreme narcissists have no empathy whatsoever. They don't take responsibility for their actions and make everyone around them feel terrible within a couple of weeks of being in their presence. It is highly unlikely that they are even remotely aware of how they are behaving, and it is even more unlikely that they are going to take a good look in the mirror and decide that they need to change.

Since you are a normal person who has feelings and genuinely cares for people, you are going to be tempted to want to help the narcissist to see the error of their ways, but this is not a good idea. It will backfire on you—their defenses will go up and they may even manage to convince you that you are the one with the problem. With an extreme narcissist, it is highly unlikely that you are going to get a fair deal, and by keeping them in your life, you are going to stay miserable.

You will need to make a decision, and you will need to make it quickly. No relationship is easy to cut off, but the easiest (and I use the word "easiest" lightly) are going to be romantic partners, colleagues, friends, and in some cases, family members. In most cases, you are not legally bound to remain in a relationship with these people. For example, you don't have joint ownership of a property, you don't own a business together, there is no dependent involved, or there is no will administration taking place. When you are free from these circumstances, escaping from such a relationship is viable. Although it is going to be a difficult decision because you might genuinely care for the person, nobody deserves to stay in a relationship that is causing them emotional damage. Breaking all contact means closing every window, door, and mailbox. Block them on all social media platforms and don't allow them to contact you by email, text, or chat. If any gap is left open, they will do everything in their power to get back in your good books. Don't read old text messages or listen to voicemails. Hearing them begging and pleading may make you feel sorry for them so that you fall into the trap they have laid for you. After you cut them off, everything they are going to say to you will come from a place of anger and manipulation, and this is not conducive to the healing process.

Although you will never completely forget about this person, you really don't want to keep them at the forefront of your memory. Therefore, it's a good idea to ask friends and family not to speak about the person or ask you if you have heard from them. You should also ask them not to provide any information about you. The dangerous thing about narcissists is that they are so charming, everyone loves them. There is a high possibility that your friends and family members won't understand why you have decided to end the relationship. More often than not, he will be in the good books of your friends and family, and he will use this as a way to get in contact with you again. He will turn up at your parents' house crying, saying he doesn't understand why you have done this to him, *"Please give me her number, I just want to talk, I just want to understand what I have done wrong, so I can fix it."* Your loved ones will need to be very stern and let him know in no uncertain terms that they will not be providing any contact information.

In the beginning stages of the breakup, it is essential that you don't spend too much time alone. First, you are going to feel lonely. You were probably in a relationship with this individual for quite some time and now you are on your own. Second, too much alone time will get you thinking, and you will start to ask yourself if you have really done the right thing. It is very important during this time to be as distracted as possible so that you don't go back.

Don't waste any time blaming yourself thinking you could have done something to change the situation. Unfortunately, this way of thinking is not new to you.

Victims of narcissist abuse are made to feel that everything that is happening to them is their fault. They spend a lot of time and energy trying to work out what they could do better or what they shouldn't have done to cause this. Please understand that it is impossible to change a narcissist—you don't have the power to do so. They can only change themselves. The only person you have the power to change is yourself, and this is what you should focus your attention on. Your thought process should be as follows: *"You were once in a terrible and unhealthy relationship; it is over and now you must focus on healing yourself."*

Another emotion you will have to deal with is the pain of knowing that your ex-partner was never really in love with you. Love is not evil—it does not cause pain and distress. This realization is very difficult to cope with, and it will make you feel unlovable. You will start to question whether you deserved to be treated in this way. As much as it hurts, thinking like this is a waste of time and energy. You have to look at the facts, regardless of a person's definition of love or whether they are capable of showing love or not, your standards dictate that you should never have been treated in this way. You will never find true love with someone with a personality disorder—they are incapable of loving anyone, not even themselves.

When you catch yourself thinking about whether your partner loved you, change your thought process and begin to tell yourself that you are worthy of love, you are valuable and there are people who will love you unconditionally, people who will not exploit you mentally and emotionally.

Educate Yourself about Mental Illness

This book has only just scratched the surface about narcissistic personality disorder. The more you know about the condition, the easier it will be for you not to end up in a similar relationship. Read books, search the internet, go to seminars, do whatever you need to do to find out as much about this disorder as possible.

The above is the only way you can become completely detached from the individual. However, if this is too extreme for you and you feel that you need to make a slow exit, there are other options which we will look at in the next chapter.

CHAPTER 8

PROTECTION STRATEGY: HOW TO SLOWLY DETACH YOURSELF FROM A NARCISSIST

It is very difficult to break up with a narcissistic partner. They have the ability to make you fall so deeply in love with them that it feels as if you are cutting out a part of your heart when you leave them. They will also use every trick they know to manipulate you into coming back. Therefore; sometimes, the best way to get out of a relationship with a narcissist is to do so slowly.

TAKE A BREAK

You can choose to manage the situation the best way you can, or you can step back and take a break from the individual. Taking a break can help you analyze the relationship from a distance and help you gain some clarity. If you are in a physically abusive relationship, taking a break is not an option, you need to cut ties with that person permanently.

Who you choose to spend your time with is important, not only because you deserve to be treated with dignity and respect, but because it is easy to be influenced by those around you. Yale University Professor Nicholas Christakis refers to this as "the ripple effect." What he means by this is that the characteristics of a person, whether good or bad, will ripple through the people they are surrounded by. Whatever you are exposed to will affect your personal development and if it is negative, expect your spirit to be infiltrated with all manner of evil. If the people you associate with are positive, you have gained something good in life.

Tell your partner that you need some space, that you are going to stay with a friend or a family member. I am warning you that he is not going to be very happy with this decision and he will attempt to do everything to stop you from leaving. Deep down, he will know you are thinking about leaving, and narcissists don't like getting dumped. However, don't fall for any of his tactics. Take a break and enjoy life without him for a while. When you make the decision to voluntarily leave, you will be able to see things differently because the shoe is on the other foot. It's not him walking out on you and leaving you in an emotional mess, you have the power now. Turn off your phone and don't allow him to contact you, it will give you the opportunity to discover what it feels like not to get abused.

DON'T GET TOO CLOSE

If you have no choice but to keep a narcissist in your life, you will need to learn the art of feeding them with a long-handled spoon. Keeping them at a distance is your safest option, but you will need to be clever about it. Narcissists are strange people—it is when you get too close to them that they begin to undervalue you. However, when you have set boundaries that you won't allow them to cross, they gain respect for you. Additionally, keeping your distance will ensure that what you say is never misinterpreted as competition or a threat to the narcissist, as they have a tendency to twist people's words and read too much into what a person is saying when they get too close to them.

Stop Giving Him Narcissistic Supply

If you find it too difficult to break up with a narcissist, make them break up with you. A narcissist will stay in a relationship when they are benefitting from it. However, as soon as the supply is cut off, they move on to the next. Their dependence on supply is their weakness, and when you are the one giving it to them, the power is in your hands. Here are two of the most powerful ways you can cut off narcissistic supply.

Show No Emotion

The narcissist feeds off your emotions—he loves to see you get angry, sad, and frustrated when he launches an attack. The goal is to show absolutely no emotion whatsoever so that it becomes glaringly obvious that he no longer has any control over you. Stop getting angry when he provokes you, don't get sad when he gives you the silent treatment, and don't react to his shaming and blaming tactics. Please understand that the narcissist has the emotional intelligence of a five-year-old, so refuse to take his behavior personally. Five-year-olds have no clue what they are doing, and to some extent, even though the narcissist is very calculating and manipulative, they have no idea of what they are doing.

SEE THEM AS OBJECTS OF STUDY

The more you understand the behavior of a narcissist, the easier it will be to outsmart them. Look at him as a social experiment, examine him and watch him as if you are zoologist observing a lion from a safe distance. Watch him without engaging with him. When you become aware of the complexities of a narcissist, you will no longer want to feed the monster when you know how dangerous this can be.

CHAPTER 9

PROTECTION STRATEGY: HOW TO CREATE BOUNDARIES WITH A NARCISSIST

In situations where you can't completely break contact with a narcissist, you can protect yourself by establishing boundaries and sticking to them. As you may well know, narcissists don't have boundaries and neither do they like it when other people put limits on their intrusions. However, if you stick to them, there is not much they can do about it but accept them. Here are some tips on how to set boundaries with narcissists.

KNOW YOUR LIMITS

Narcissists can be very rude and aggressive. They will call you names and bully you, especially if you don't jump when they tell you to. If you are not willing to tolerate name-calling, bullying, and rudeness, tell them. For example, if you are in the middle of a conversation and they start acting up, say: *"Listen if you keep acting the way you are, I will put an end to this conversation until you are capable of showing me some respect.*" You don't need to give an explanation or a reason. If they choose not to take you seriously and they continue, say: "*As I mentioned, your rudeness is unacceptable, and I am not willing to talk to you when you act like this, goodbye.*" Either hang up the phone or walk out of the room. Don't engage in any further conversation with them and don't allow them to respond. The more decisively and quickly you act the easier it will be to disarm the narcissist.

The narcissist is likely to continue with their abuse. They may try to call you or follow you and attempt to convince you that you are being unfair or that you are going over the top. They will try a number of different approaches to see if they can confuse, intimidate, or get you to feel guilty about your decision.

While their begging and the pressure they are putting you under is uncomfortable, your boundaries are not up for negotiation. Sticking to your decision will lead you to feel stronger, less overwhelmed, safer, and calmer.

HAVE A PLAN OF ESCAPE

You don't need permission to leave an unhealthy interaction with another person. There are a variety of techniques you can use to get out of a conversation. For example, you can take a quick look at your watch and say, "*Oh my goodness, is that the time, I need to leave.*" Then walk out.

What you are saying you are late for is irrelevant. With a narcissist, every minute you allow them to abuse you is one more minute you allow them to get into your head.

Or you can glance at your phone and say, *"I'm really sorry, but I've got an important call I need to take."* You can do this whether your phone is ringing or not.

Or, since you already know the narcissist's character, set an alarm on your phone in advance and once the alarm goes off, excuse yourself.

YOU DECIDE WHAT YOU WANT TO TALK ABOUT

Politicians are good at doing this. When they are being interviewed, you rarely hear them answering the question they were asked. They talk about what they want to talk about. In the same way, when a narcissist asks you a question that you are not comfortable with, change the subject. If they ask you what's going on in your relationship or how you are handling your finances, and they have a bad habit of criticizing you for the way you spend your money or conduct yourself in a relationship, why put yourself through that again? Instead, change the tide of the conversation and start talking about something you know the narcissist loves discussing. For example, you could ask them how they learned to manage their money so well, and if they have found the secrets to the perfect relationship. Although they are now going to spend your time talking about themselves, at least you are no longer the focus of the conversation.

DON'T GIVE TOO MUCH INFORMATION

Limit the amount of private information you share with a narcissist. The less they know about you, the less ammunition they have to use against you. If they have something negative to say about what you are doing say, *"I am confident in the decisions I have made."* Or, *"I have taken note of your opinion."*

NAME WHAT THEY ARE DOING

Narcissists are always trying to see how much they can get away with and will push the limits in a relationship. They want to be the center of attention at all times. One way to put a stop to this is to say, *"I notice that any time I start talking about myself you cut me off to talk about you."* Or, *"That sounded like you were trying to put me down."* You don't need to say anything else after that, just state the facts and leave it alone. What they say afterward is irrelevant. You have put your mark on the conversation by letting them know that you know what they are up to.

TAKE THE FOCUS OFF THEM

Narcissists live for attention—they love being praised, complimented, and admired. When you engage in conversation with them, they make sure they are the main focus. What you are feeling, experiencing, or going through is irrelevant to them. Whatever they believe, say, or need at that moment is their main priority, and they expect you to agree with them. To avoid being swept into the tide, perform a mental check every so often when you are communicating with a narcissist. Take note of what you are thinking, feeling, and wanting. If you find it too difficult to do this in the moment, when you have left the conversation, go over it and remember how you were thinking and feeling at the time. When you are aware of what is going on, you reduce the power of the narcissist to suffocate you with their agenda. If you ever attend a self-help group, you will hear the term *"gray rock"* when they are referring to narcissists. This means toning down how much you allow yourself to care about a narcissist. For that period of time you are with them, become as impenetrable as a rock. This is a way of disassociating yourself in an emotionally unsafe environment. The gray rock approach is a reminder that you are not going to give them your energy, neither are you going to fully engage with them, you reserve this type of normal behavior for safe people. Reacting emotionally or showing vulnerability around a narcissist gives them the green light to continue to abuse you even more.

Narcissists enjoy getting an emotional reaction out of people; in their perverted mind, it lets them know that they exist. By showing that they have an effect on you, you encourage their unhealthy intrusions and behaviors. Of course, narcissists are experts at getting people to react to their foolishness, so there are going to be times when you slip up no matter how hard you try not to. However, when you catch yourself, change the subject or excuse yourself.

REALIZE THAT YOU WILL HAVE TO KEEP SETTING BOUNDARIES WITH A NARCISSIST

In the majority of cases, when you are dealing with normal people, you can set boundaries once, and they will abide by them and you won't have to set them again. This is not the case with narcissists. They will continuously push against the boundaries you set in an attempt to wear you down. Therefore, if you want to keep those boundaries, you will need to keep re-establishing them.

Don't Be Too Hard on Yourself

If you fail to set healthy boundaries or you slip up every once in a while, don't be too hard on yourself. Narcissists are very skilled individuals, and in most cases, this is someone you have been dealing with for years and you have only just decided to put your foot down. In such instances, you will have years of vulnerability to deal with, and that is a lot to get over. Allow yourself room for error, and when you realize you have messed up, ask yourself what you will do differently next time.

Focus on Improving Yourself

Narcissists care about appearance and image, so whoever they are with, they expect them to act in a way that validates them, this is typically at your expense. You have to decide who you are going to be around a narcissist, ask yourself:

- Do I want to feel confident and strong? Or overwhelmed and small?
- What am I standing for right now?
- How can I give myself the utmost respect in this situation?

The answers you provide will give you some important insight into the person you want to be at that moment.

REMEMBER WHO YOU ARE DEALING WITH

Narcissists are extremely needy, and underneath their fake exterior, they feel inferior and empty. The wall of confidence they have built around themselves is to hide how they really feel from the rest of the world. When you know the truth about a narcissist, it allows you to see them for who they really are as opposed to the bully who thinks they know everything and has the power to reduce you to a whimpering five-year-old. Remind yourself that the narcissist has a hard life, and the constant need for approval must be extremely draining. In no way am I suggesting that their issues justify their controlling and abusive behavior, but what it does do is remind you not to take what they do personally and, to a certain extent, have compassion on them.

ENFORCE THE CONSEQUENCES

If the narcissist is not willing to respect your boundaries, you will need to enforce consequences. This is the only way you will let them know that you are serious. Before you meet up with a narcissist, decide what the consequences are going to be if your boundaries are ignored or violated. What you don't want to happen is that you try to work out what the consequences are going to be in the middle of a situation. Once you have told the narcissist what the consequences are going to be, enforce them immediately, don't give any explanation, don't waste time, just do it. If not, you will reap the consequences of not enforcing them, which is playing the narcissist's game.

When you start setting boundaries, narcissists will up their attack. They may start spreading rumors and gossip about you or threaten to disown you. This is the risk you take when choosing to have a narcissist in your life. You will also need to think about these potential consequences that your boundaries could lead to. It may need to be the case that you choose your battles wisely instead of getting them so angry that they have a personal vendetta against you.

PROTECTION STRATEGY: HOW TO STOP AN ARGUMENT WITH A NARCISSIST

Object constancy is when a person finds it difficult to have positive and negative feelings at the same time. For example, when a narcissist is ready to have a fight, they can be extremely vicious because all they understand at the time are their feelings of anger and resentment. This can lead to an argument about something seemingly insignificant turning into something fierce. If the narcissist is violent, the smallest issue can cause them to strike their partner or start throwing things.

Depending on their sub-type, narcissists have the tendency to be very fragile. They get offended easily and will accuse their partner of being selfish or disrespectful if they dare to put their needs first. In their eyes, the world revolves around them so if their partner focuses on anything else, they see it as a direct insult. Psychologists have yet to work out whether this behavior is conscious or not, and if they actually mean to cause the harm they do when they fly into a rage.

EXPECT A SEVERE ALTERCATION

Fighting with a narcissist is not like anything you will ever experience. Because of their hypersensitive nature and lack of empathy, they are wired to be abusive; therefore, it is normal for them to have zero understanding for someone else's needs and take offense at the slightest misunderstanding. Narcissistic rage has levels—they might give their partner the silent treatment for hours or have a screaming match in which they verbally abuse their partner with hurtful names. Or they will just walk out and find someone else to sleep with in the coldest and calculating manner. If you find yourself in this position with a narcissist, there are some strategies you can implement to deescalate the situation.

DON'T GET INTO AN ARGUMENT ABOUT RIGHT OR WRONG

You are wasting your time if you think you are ever going to win an argument with a narcissist; even if they are in the wrong, they are never going to admit it. They will want you to take responsibility for every negative emotion you are feeling because they are totally dependent on keeping up the image that they are perfect and can do nothing wrong.

TRY TO EMPATHIZE WITH HOW THEY ARE FEELING

Most people who are in a relationship with a narcissist have a lot of empathy anyway. However, even the most empathetic person finds it difficult to have empathy for someone who is bashing them with insults. If you find that you have been backed into a corner, one way to calm a narcissist down is to say something like, *"What I did must have been very hurtful for you, I can understand why you are so angry."* In this way, you are letting them know that you are taking responsibility for your actions, even though you know you have done nothing wrong.

You Are in This Together

Do not use language such as *"you"* or *"I,"* instead say *"we,"* in this way, you are indirectly saying that you are also to blame for what is taking place. The narcissist is going to be extremely angry because you had the audacity to defend yourself, so to prevent the argument from escalating, remind them that you are in this together.

Ask about Something They are Interested in

Narcissists love to talk about themselves or to display how much they know about a certain subject. So, in the same way you would distract a baby with a toy, you can distract the narcissist with a new conversation to steer the conversation out of an argument. This probably won't work in the middle of a screaming row; it is more effective if you do it before the argument has escalated or after the flames have died down.

Another strategy is to ask the narcissist for advice. They take pride in the fact that they have reduced you to a dependent child who can't do anything unless they sanction it. It will make the narcissist feel that they are the only person you can go to and it will make them feel superior.

Don't Take the Bait

Since the narcissist believes you have severely hurt them, they will want to get revenge on you. To do so, they will throw everything they think you've ever done to them back in your face, and on top of that, remind you of how selfish you are being now. Their main aim is to get you to react emotionally, so your best response is to ignore the comments. By responding, you will simply encourage another argument, which is what you are trying to avoid.

Don't Expect an Apology

A narcissist will never admit they are in the wrong, so don't even ask for an apology. The most important thing is that you know that you didn't do anything to deserve what just took place. Trying to get the narcissist to see things from your point of view is a waste of time and energy. It is also important that you don't ask them to process what just happened. They will feel very uncomfortable reminding themselves that they started an argument over something so trivial, so the best thing to do is to leave it alone.

CHAPTER 11

PROTECTION STRATEGY: PRACTICE GIVING BALANCED LOVE

The narcissist feeds off their victim's fear, and the victim feels that in order to gain the narcissist's approval, to gain their love and to feel worthy, they must never disappoint the narcissist. The narcissist takes full advantage of their victim's needs and desire to be loved, wanted, seen as loving, kind, nice, and unselfish by them. The narcissists view these traits as a sign of inferiority and weakness and will take every opportunity to disrupt their partner's feelings of security and self-worth and replace them with self-blame, self-doubt, and fear.

To overcome this, the victim must take responsibility for their own healing and choose to put themselves first. They must understand that it's impossible to put a stop to what the narcissist is doing if they don't work to change themselves from within. This is essential because, in reality, the way you treat yourself is the only thing that human beings have complete and total control over. To start, here are some strategies that the victim can implement.

- Create an emotional detachment from the need to rescue the narcissist from their self-sabotaging behaviors.
- Refuse to allow the narcissist to treat you like a punching bag.
- Refuse to depend on the narcissist for safety, feelings of value, and self-worth.
- Realize that the narcissist will never care for you unless they first relinquish their false sense of reality.
- Understand that trying to get validation from a narcissist is like attempting to get blood out of a stone.

The right actions will begin to follow once you reach this place; however, it is not going to be easy, especially if you have been in the relationship for several years. Old ingrained habits will keep coming up, and you will need to work to shut them down. The victim must learn to completely emotionally detach themselves from the narcissist but do so in a loving way. There is no need to stoop to the same level as the narcissist during this process, which will feed into what they want. Remember, the narcissist wants to get a rise out of you, so if you get angry and start hurling insults at them, they have won. The narcissist will enjoy the fact that you are giving them an excuse to continue arguing with you.

To detach yourself means that you have shifted your focus from taking care of the needs, wants, and desires of the narcissist onto yourself. Instead of trying to rescue them, you are now rescuing yourself. You are rescuing your self-respect and sanity and cultivating the self-acceptance and compassion that will free yourself from toxic behavioral patterns.

It is essential to understand that you have no power to change the narcissist. Unless they decide that the way they are living is not benefiting them, they will never change. Until this happens, you will never be in a safe place with a narcissist, so don't listen to what they have to say. Narcissists can talk a good game, but their actions will determine whether they are serious or not.

CHAPTER 12

PROTECTION STRATEGY: CUT ALL PSYCHIC CORDS

f you are not sure what a psychic cord is (also known as an etheric cord), let me explain. Have you ever gotten so deeply involved in a conversation with someone that long after the discussion has ended, you are still emotionally involved in the other person's issues? A lot of empaths experience this due to the sensitive nature of their spirit. It feels as if you are still having the conversation because it is continuously playing in your head. This is how the majority of people feel the effects of a psychic cord.

Psychic cords connect you to loved ones including friends, family, romantic partners, and pets. They assist in transmitting the exchange of feelings, thoughts, and energy. When the connection is healthy, the cord will transmit telepathic information and love between two people and intensify the connection between them both. However, when you are in a relationship with a narcissist who abuses you, this connection is not healthy. In your case, it is important that the cord is severed.

UNHEALTHY PSYCHIC CORDS – THE NEGATIVE EFFECTS

Unhealthy psychic cords drain your energy. They will challenge your mental health and make you feel physically sick. Psychic cords are typically created with people that you have empathetic feelings towards. It is common for healers to experience this with their clients. When a mother looks after her sick child, she transmits some of her energy to assist in the healing process. Caregivers, nurses, and teachers have a tendency to experience unhealthy psychic cords. Any type of co-dependent relationship will be bound by unhealthy psychic cords. People will cut these cords in an effort to release themselves from negative energy that no longer benefits them.

Ethers are like auras—they help to maintain the physical body and can also assist in connecting with spiritual entities that are on a higher plane. If you were to describe a psychic cord physically, it is compared to an umbilical cord. In a loving and healthy relationship, this cord extends through the heart chakra and good energy is exchanged back and forth. In an unbalanced or unhealthy relationship, this cord extends through the naval area or the solar plexus where energy is leached between two people. Those who make you feel sympathy or pity and you are constantly concerned for them may have a cord attached to you and you are not aware of it. This can prevent good things from taking place in your life because you are continuously caught up in their negative energy. It is important that you are aware of how someone else's negative energy can affect your life. In the case of an unhealthy relationship in which you have been abused, it is essential that the cord is severed and never reconnected.

How to Cut Psychic Cords

Although you have just been through months or possibly years of abuse, it is essential that the psychic cord you have with your ex-partner is cut with love. When you dissolve the connection, you are sending it back to the Creator or whatever it is that you believe in has divine power over you. Release any fears or judgments you may have about having a psychic cord with such an abusive person and about any way that you may have participated. Once the cord has been cut, your vitality and energy will be restored immediately. You will clear your emotions and free your mind so that you can focus on moving forward with your life. The results are typically subtle, but sometimes they can have a massively positive effect on you. When unhealthy psychic cords are released, you open the door to new and unlimited opportunities in your life. Here are a few techniques you can use to cut unhealthy psychic cords.

- Stand with your arms stretched out in front of you and then cross your arms over each other as if you are making a large X shape.
- Starting with your hands positioned at your groin area (root chakra), slightly move one hand a couple of inches up from the body. Keep raising your arm slowly until it is raised over the top of your head.

- Call upon the archangel Michael to sever the psychic cord in the purest and highest of ways.
- Meditate on cutting the cord and ask that any lessons learned from the experience are revealed to you. Send forgiveness to your ex-partner, visualize that the cords have severed their purpose and have been turned back into love.

Spend some time in gratitude that you have severed these cords, do some deep breathing exercises, and start thinking about how you can move forward in life.

CHAPTER 13:

PROTECTION STRATEGY: RECLAIM YOUR LIFE

Emotional abuse is deeply damaging, and without going through the healing process, you make yourself even more vulnerable to entering into the same type of relationship. You have been violated psychologically, and you will experience anxiety, depression, dissociation, feelings of low self-esteem, low self-worth, nightmares, and flashbacks. As mentioned in chapter 6, it is essential that you seek counseling to assist you in the healing process; however, there are strategies you can implement in your daily life that will help you to move forward.

YOGA

The effects of trauma live in the body, yoga is a combination of physical activity and mindfulness that help to establish and restore balance. Research has proven that yoga alleviates anxiety and depression, it improves symptoms of post-traumatic stress disorder in victims of domestic violence, boosts self-esteem, and improves body image. Yoga involves a series of powerful movements that compensate for the feelings of powerlessness that victims of abuse are left with.

Dr. Bessel Van der Kolk has spent years studying the benefits of yoga, and he believes that it allows traumatized victims to take back ownership of their bodies. Trauma robs abuse victims of a sense of safety, and yoga helps them reconnect through the use of bodily sensations.

MEDITATION

Trauma disrupts the area in the brain responsible for memory, learning, emotion regulation, and planning. Research has found that meditation benefits the same areas of the brain that are affected by trauma such as the hippocampus, the amygdala, and the prefrontal cortex. Meditation gives abuse victims their psyche back. It heals the brain and allows them to respond to life from a place of empowerment instead of a place of trauma.

Daily meditation practice strengthens the neural pathways in the brain and boosts grey matter density in areas of the brain related to the fight or flight response and emotion regulation. Meditation also allows you to become aware of your need to make contact with your abuser. When victims are not aware of this, they make impulse decisions which usually leads to them returning to the relationship. It also makes you more aware of your emotions in general.

ANCHOR YOURSELF

In general, emotional abuse survivors have been gaslighted into believing that they were imagining the abuse they were experiencing. It is essential that you start anchoring yourself into the reality of the fact that you were abused, but you are no longer in that abusive situation. It is common for abuse victims to idealize the relationship they were in and spend time thinking about what could have been if only they were capable of pleasing their partner. Connecting to reality also helps when struggling with mixed emotions towards your abuser. As mentioned, one of the strategies of the narcissist is to show affection and withdraw it, and it is the affectionate side of the narcissist that victims are drawn to. The narcissist seeks to erode the reality of their victim, but once you are reconnected with your reality, you are able to see your abuser for who he truly is.

Survivors are extremely vulnerable when they get out of an abusive relationship; their abusers will revert back to displaying their loving and affectionate side to manipulate them into coming back. This is why it is essential that you block phone calls and texts and any other form of contact so that he has no way of getting into your head. This allows you to connect to what really happened to you instead of allowing him to convince you that your version of events is incorrect.

To start the anchoring process, make a list of ten of the most abusive incidents that took place during your relationship. When you get tempted to reconnect with your abuser, read this list and remind yourself of how evil he was to you, how he degraded you and made you feel less than human. You can also write down statements about how he made you feel such as: *"My abuser made me feel that I wasn't worth anything." "My abuser made me feel depressed," "My abuser made me feel that I was stupid." "My abuser made me feel as if I was getting what I deserved and that no one could ever love me the way he did."* Remind yourself of these feelings any time you are tempted to pick up the phone and call him or go to his house and see him. Ask yourself whether it feels good for someone to make you believe this about yourself. The more you remember the negative feelings associated with the relationship, the easier it will be to stay away.

WORK WITH YOUR INNER CHILD, SELF-SOOTHING

You didn't just happen to fall into an abusive relationship, there are some deep-rooted issues within you that have led you to this point in your life, and they typically stem from childhood. Through therapy, you will discover that there were some fundamental needs that were not met during childhood. In attempting to fill that void, you settled for an abusive relationship. Once you discover what that void is, it is essential that you learn what is required to fill it, so that you do not leave yourself vulnerable to enter into another abusive relationship. During the healing process, you will need to be extremely compassionate with yourself because of what you went through as a child, and the abuse you have endured is not your fault. Abuse has the power to open up old wounds that were never healed. The belief system that you have never felt good enough has always been a part of your psyche. Your abusive partner simply confirmed how you have always felt. When you are healing, it is essential that you change the narrative that is taking place in your mind, which is important in general, but even more so when you are recovering from abuse. Self-compassion can be the most powerful form of compassion, so it is important that you are gentle with yourself during this time.

When you start feeling these negative emotions, comfort yourself as if you were speaking to a child who is being bullied in the playground. Tell yourself that you are the opposite of everything the negative self-chatter is trying to speak to your mind. You can say things such as, *"I am worthy of love," "I am special," "I deserve great things to happen in my life."* Over time, you will learn to stop blaming yourself and begin to overcome the toxic shame you have been subjected to. When you are judging yourself for what happened, you are more likely to indulge in self-sabotaging behaviors. But you can erase this by showing yourself compassion and reminding yourself that you are worthy of being kind and caring for yourself.

EXERCISE

Whether it's going for long intensive walks, going for a jog, joining a dance class, or joining the gym, incorporating exercise into your daily routine will really help during the healing process. If you don't have any motivation, don't try and do too much at once; for example, you can start off by going for a ten-minute walk and then increase it as time goes on. Exercise lowers cortisol levels and releases endorphins, which helps to replace the biochemical addiction you developed with your abuser with something that will benefit you. This addiction was formed through chemicals such as cortisol, dopamine, serotonin, and adrenaline which strengthen the bond with your abuser and form the cycle of highs and lows. Exercise allows you to build a wall of strength and resilience after leaving an abuser. It also helps to eliminate a lot of the physical problems associated with the abuse such as weight gain, sleep problems, premature aging, and a depleted immune system.

PUT UNHEALTHY COPING STRATEGIES TO BED

You did everything possible to try to keep your narcissistic partner happy and to keep him from flying into a fit of rage. Your days were spent walking on eggshells—you learned how to be silent and submissive, to question your every move, and to start all your conversations with the words, *"I'm sorry."* You learned how to dodge bullets and avoid landmines and act as if parts of your dreams, desires, and needs didn't exist. You learned how to devalue yourself and accept treatment from another human being that was totally unacceptable. The mental anguish you had to go through just to experience even a little bit of peace and keep yourself, and maybe your children, safe from harm was astounding. All these terrible things you had to learn were not only unhealthy, but in a normal relationship, they are not skills that will serve you well; therefore, you must learn new and normal habits that will benefit you in a healthy relationship. Unlearning old habits involves a system of self-monitoring; there are two types, qualitative and quantitative.

- Qualitative Monitoring: This involves being attentive to the old habits that you are engaging in—what do they look like and how do they make you feel?

- Quantitative Monitoring: This involves counting the old habits that don't serve you to monitor how many times you are engaging in them throughout the day.

Although both types of self-monitoring are effective, quantitative monitoring is most beneficial because for the first time you can accurately measure how you are behaving and the triggers that cause these bad habits to resurface. Previously, you may have had a slight idea of how bad your problem was, but now you can actually see it as well as have something to measure your progress by.

It is important that you establish a system for the self-monitoring process. It should include what you are monitoring, how you are going to record your observations, and how often the monitoring process will take place. For example, one of the most common coping strategies for women in an abusive relationship is normalizing the abuse. They do this by convincing themselves that they deserve the treatment, or even by telling themselves that other women go through this too, so it must just be what men do. It is impossible to monitor every single one of your thoughts, sometimes you are not consciously aware that you are thinking like this. However, there are going to be times when you catch yourself, and it is at this point that you should record the information. There doesn't need to be anything complicated about this process, simply carry a notebook with you and jot down the information. If you realize that something triggered you to start thinking this way, write that down too. Write down the date, the time, the thought, what triggered you, and how you felt when you started to think this way.

LEARN TO LOVE YOURSELF

This might sound cliché, but it is essential if you are going to move on with your life and eventually get into a healthy relationship. When you love yourself, you know who you are and what you stand for. It is impossible for anyone to come along and try to convince you that you are anything less than the best! When you develop a certain level of confidence and self-worth, nothing can shake you. Here are some tips on how to love yourself after an abusive relationship.

- **Get in Shape:** When you look good, you feel good! We have already discussed the benefits of exercise, so looking good is simply an added bonus. Make a decision not only to improve your health but to transform your body. Whatever your ideal weight and shape are, aim for that.

- **Change Your Wardrobe:** Once you have achieved your ideal body shape, treat yourself to some new clothes. You don't need to break the bank but buy some signature pieces that are really going to make you feel good about yourself.

- **Have Fun Alone:** Take one day out of the week and do something that you enjoy. A lot of abuse victims have difficulty being alone, which is why they are such easy prey for abusers. Spending time alone will teach you how to enjoy your own company. Things you could do might include, going to the movies, out to dinner, or finding a new hobby.

- **Try Something New:** Do things that you wouldn't normally do. Try something new and crazy like skydiving or bungee jumping. That's a bit extreme, but you know yourself better than anyone else, so you can choose something that you know will add an element of surprise to your life.

- **Go on Vacation:** Even if you don't make it a regular thing, take a vacation somewhere. Go to a country that's completely out of your comfort zone. If you are not brave enough to go alone, invite a friend. Experience a different culture, new food, different activities, and have fun.

- **Journal:** Journaling is a good way to release any negative emotions you are feeling. It is also a good way of tracking your progress. When you come out of an abusive relationship, you are going to have more bad days than good ones. Some days are going to be better than others; however, after some time, you will notice that your emotions will begin to stabilize.

- **Learn to Say No:** Being submissive is a survival mechanism for women in abusive relationships. You would never dare say no to your partner in fear of what might happen. However, now that you are not in an abusive relationship, it is important that you don't carry this submissive nature into your friendships or feel as if you need to say yes to everyone to please them. This will rob you of your energy and time to yourself.

- **Celebrate Your Accomplishments:** No matter how small you think the accomplishment is, celebrate it. Going through a whole day without thinking about your ex is an accomplishment and being consistent with your daily exercise routine is an accomplishment. Pay attention to these things and treat yourself for it.

- **Challenge Yourself:** Is there anything that you have always wanted to do but you have never gotten around to doing it? Make a list of these things and start doing them. You may have always wanted to compete in a triathlon or to get some additional qualifications. Decide that whatever you put your mind to, you are going to achieve.

- **Learn to Trust Yourself:** Before you got into an abusive relationship, your instincts told you that something wasn't right, but you chose to ignore them and pursue the relationship in the hopes that things would get better. Familiarize yourself with that feeling, because any time something isn't right, that is how you will feel, and this isn't just about relationships, it's in all areas of your life.

CHAPTER 14

DATING AGAIN

Life does go on after a trauma, and it's essential that you go through all stages of the healing process before you get into another relationship because you don't want to carry any baggage with you. Whether the relationship was abusive or not, people will typically leave one relationship and go straight into another one because they want to fill the void. This is a big mistake. What ends up happening, especially in abusive relationships, is you go from one abusive relationship to the next because that is the energy you are giving off. It's like abusers have some type of radar and they can spot a victim a mile off. However, you can avoid this by taking the time to heal and become a whole person again. When you are confident, and your self-esteem is high, you will attract the right man into your life. Another mistake people make after they have been hurt is avoiding getting into another relationship altogether. There is a big difference between avoiding an abusive relationship and falling in love. Falling in love is a risk. Even if the guy ticks all the boxes, you know he is not a narcissist, and he doesn't have abusive tendencies, you still don't know where the relationship will go. You just have to follow your heart.

The best way to get back onto the dating scene is to start slow; don't rush into things. Here are some tips you can apply to help you move forward in your love life.

- Look out for red flags (we discussed this in chapter 5), listen to your gut instincts, and hit the road if he begins to show any signs of narcissism.

- Keep your options open, don't jump into a relationship with the first man that ticks all the boxes. Spend time dating, get to know a few guys and make sure that you choose the best one.

- Don't make judgments based on your previous relationships. You are dealing with an entirely different person now. If a man feels as if he is being judged based on what someone else did to you, he will be very reluctant to move forward in the relationship. It is important to remember that narcissists are a rare breed; experts believe that only 10% of the population are narcissists, and the percentage is probably higher based on those who haven't been diagnosed. However, when you are bold and full of confidence, it is highly unlikely that you are going to run into a narcissist or any other type of abusive male because they look for a specific type of woman and that isn't you anymore.

- Get a second opinion. A great indicator as to whether a person is a good fit for you is if your friends and family like him. The people closest to you have your best interests at heart—they are capable of seeing things that you might miss. If they like him, move ahead, but if they have compelling reasons why they don't like him, you might need to go back to the drawing board.

- Don't sleep with him until you have both made a serious commitment to each other; sex complicates things. If he is not willing to wait, you know that he is not a keeper.

Remember, regardless of what you were told as a child, or what your former narcissistic partner made you believe, you are awesome, beautiful, vivacious, you have a wonderful destiny, and you have skills and talents to bless people with. You deserve to be loved unconditionally, and one day you will find the relationship of your dreams and live happily ever after!

CHAPTER 15

FREQUENTLY ASKED QUESTIONS ABOUT NARCISSISTS

There is so much more to say about narcissism that it's impossible to fit it into this book. Therefore, I have included a FAQ section so that I can touch on a few more subjects, even though I am not going into too much depth.

What is passing the hot potato?

Because narcissists don't like feeling uncomfortable, they use this method to dodge how they are feeling. It's a game they play, and the hot potato is their feelings. Typically, people drop hot potatoes, but in this instance, they pass it along. Someone who likes to feel as if they have everything under control likes to use this method, it's a form of deflection. If you have a narcissistic boss, you will find that he questions everything that you do. They nit-pick, and you start to think that you are incapable of doing anything right.

What they are attempting to do is get rid of their feelings of vulnerability by insinuating that you are the one doing everything wrong, when deep down, they feel as if they can't do anything right.

How do I get around the hot potato pass?

By calling it out. You will know how the narcissist is really feeling by the type of questions they ask. This works even better if you're an empath because you will be able to sense their energy and how they are feeling. So, you can say something like, *"Has something happened to make you feel like this today? Something is telling me that you might not be too sure about the project we are working on, or is there something going on with this project that you haven't told me about?"* This will completely disarm the narcissist because they will know they have been called out. At this point, they will either come clean or walk away from the conversation.

What is the one question I can ask to prove that someone is a narcissist?

There are a few questions you can ask, but the type of question that works the best is to ask them about their previous relationships. If they don't take any responsibility for a breakup or feel as if there was nothing they could have done in a relationship to make things better, you know you are dealing with a narcissist. As mentioned throughout this book, narcissists don't take responsibility for anything, they believe that they are always in the right and that they are incapable of doing anything wrong. You probably won't find out the extent of their narcissism from one question, but their answer will give you some insight and you can start probing from there.

WHAT IS STEALTH CONTROL?

Narcissists use this all the time. It is when they engineer circumstances to ensure that they get what they want. Narcissists have a phobia of asking for things directly because they are scared of rejection and it puts them in a position of vulnerability. To avoid this, they will simply make things happen. An example would be your boyfriend turning up at your house with two concert tickets. The concert is literally starting in an hour, you don't even have time to process what's going on, and you are being dragged out of your house to this concert with no preparation or planning. However, when you suggest going to a movie or going out to dinner, your partner is never interested. The reason being is that he wants to have full control over your life and that includes your social activities.

WHAT IS FLUCTUATING EMPATHY?

In the right conditions, narcissists do have the ability to show empathy. Studies have found that when they are prompted to think about a situation from another person's point of view, they are capable of doing so. It is also important to mention that there are some situations where they won't show any empathy, hence the term "fluctuating empathy."

How does the twin fantasy work?

Basically, it is when the narcissist mirrors the behavior of an empath. When they see that the empath is getting the admiration and the attention that they crave, they immediately go into twin mode and begin to imitate the empath's nature. However, this should never be mistaken as real empathy in that moment—it is their way of getting their narcissistic supply. Narcissists are simply very good at acting.

CONCLUSION

Thank you for taking the time to read this book. Narcissism is a subject that is very dear to my heart and I hope that you now have a deeper understanding of the condition. It is more than just a word we use in casual conversation to describe someone who is full of themselves. Narcissism is a very rare personality disorder that shouldn't be seen in any other way. A person who is slightly unkind or jealous every once in a while is not a narcissist, they're just not having the best of days. This is especially true if they realize that they are in the wrong and they apologize to the person they have hurt or offended for what they have done. However, if the individual does not acknowledge their wrong and believes that their behavior was totally okay, you could have a narcissist on your hands.

Although narcissism is a mental condition that a person has no control over, that doesn't mean you should tolerate their behavior, especially if they are not willing to change and get the help that they need. It isn't easy to get a narcissist out of your life, but it is absolutely necessary if you are ever going to live a fulfilling life.

Narcissism is actually a heart-breaking condition and I wouldn't wish it on my worst enemy. Although it is spoken about in such a negative light because of the damage that it causes other people, we forget to acknowledge the fact that if these people don't get the help that they need, they will end up lonely and depressed for the rest of their lives. What's even sadder is that this is not something that happens often because narcissists don't think that there is anything wrong with them—they truly believe that they are not the ones with the problem.

Even though you have come to the end of this book, if you are currently in a relationship with a narcissist, it's not the end for you and there is still a long way to go in terms of detaching yourself from the situation. So before you go, I want to refresh your memory with these key points:

- A true narcissist must be diagnosed with narcissistic personality disorder (NPD).
- There are fewer female narcissists than there are men.
- Approximately 10% of the population suffer from NPD.
- There are levels of narcissism ranging from mild to severe.
- The main characteristics of a narcissist are delusions of grandeur, an inflated sense of self-importance and a constant desire to be at the forefront of everything. However, these are just some of the most common characteristics, they are many and varied.
- There are categories of narcissists, including toxic, vulnerable, and classic.
- Toxic narcissists are very dangerous and have been closely linked to sociopaths and psychopaths.

- Narcissists are master manipulators, they are highly skilled emotional abusers.
- The majority of narcissists end up alone because they refuse to accept that they have a problem.
- Narcissists are very attracted to empaths, they make an extremely toxic combination.
- The cause of narcissism has never been confirmed; however, there is a possibility that it could stem from childhood, it is also possible that it is genetic.
- Underneath the mask, narcissists are extremely insecure with low self-esteem, they need to be affirmed constantly.
- You cannot change or fix a narcissist; they must see that there is something wrong with them in order for them to go and get the help that they need.
- It can be very difficult to find the strength to leave a narcissistic relationship. Once you do get out, you will need to seek professional help to heal from the emotional abuse you have endured.
- Narcissists use gaslighting to emotionally abuse their victims, it is a very severe and damaging form of abuse that involves manipulating the emotions and thoughts of a person to the extent that they begin to question their own sanity.
- Do not allow a narcissist to make you feel guilty about leaving them, it is essential that you get out of the relationship for your own emotional well-being.

By educating yourself as much as you can on narcissism, you have taken the first steps in the direction to total freedom. Not only will this information assist you in getting out of the relationship you are currently in, but it will ensure that you are never entrapped in this type of partnership again.

I wish you every blessing and success for the future.

THANKS FOR READING!

I really hope you enjoyed this book, and most of all got more value from it than you had to give.

It would mean a lot to me if you left an Amazon review—I will reply to all questions asked!

Simply find this book on Amazon, scroll to the reviews section, and click "Write a customer review".

Or Scan the QR Code on Your Phone:

Be sure to check out my email list, where I am constantly adding tons of value. The best way to currently get on the list is by visiting www.pristinepublish.com/empathbonus and entering your email.

Here I'll provide actionable information that aims to improve your enjoyment of life. I'll update you on my latest books, and I'll even send free e-books that I think you'll find useful.

Kindest regards,

Judy Dyer

ALSO BY
Judy Dyer

Grasp a better understanding of your gift and how you can embrace every part of it so that your life is enriched day by day.

Visit: www.pristinepublish.com/judy

Or Scan the QR Code on Your Phone: